Irrigation Impacts on Rural Poverty in India

Macro and Micro Evidence

Susanto Kumar Beero
A. Narayanamoorthy

CONCEPT PUBLISHING COMPANY PVT. LTD.
NEW DELHI-110059

ISBN-13: 978-93-86682-52-9

First Published in 2019

Published and Printed by

Concept Since 1974

Concept Publishing Company Pvt. Ltd.
A/15-16, Commercial Block, Mohan Garden,
New Delhi-110059 (INDIA)
T : 91 11 25351460, 91 11 25351794
E : publishing@conceptpub.com; *W* : www.conceptpub.com

Cataloging in Publication Data--Courtesy: D.K. Agencies (P) Ltd. <docinfo@dkagencies.com>

Beero, Susanto Kumar, author.
Irrigation impacts on rural poverty in India : macro and micro evidence / Susanto Kumar Beero, A. Narayanamoorthy.
pages cm
Study conducted in Pudukkottai District of Tamil Nadu, India.
Includes bibliographical references and index.
ISBN 99789386682529

1. Irrigation—Economic aspects--India—Pudukkottai (District) 2. Rural poor—India—Pudukkottai (District) 3. Agriculture—Economic aspects—India—Pudukkottai (District) I. Narayanamoorthy, A., author. II. Title.

LCC HD1741.I42P83 2019 | DDC 338.10954 23

Preface

The impacts of irrigation development on various parameters of agricultural development including productivity and production of crops have been well documented by various studies carried out in different countries including India. Irrigation development also helps to reduce the rural poverty in a sustained manner by increasing employment opportunities and wage rate for agricultural labourers where the incidence of poverty is reportedly very high. However, till late 1990s, the role of irrigation development in reducing the rural poverty has not been analysed by treating it as an important explanatory variable in the analysis on rural poverty. In this study, keeping this in view, we have analysed the impact of irrigation development on rural poverty using both macro and micro-level primary data. The major highlight of this study is that it has analysed the source-wise impact of irrigation on rural poverty which is seldom observed in the existing literature on irrigation and poverty.

This study was carried out with the financial assistance (Ph.D., Fellowship) from NABARD, Mumbai through NABARD Chair Professor Scheme. This NABARD Chair Professor Scheme (one among the five Chairs instituted at the national level) was awarded to Prof. A Narayanamoorthy by recognizing his significant research contributions to irrigation and agricultural economics by NABARD, Mumbai. We profusely thank NABARD for providing financial assistance for carrying out this study.

We would like to thank our colleagues Dr. B. Dharmalingam, Dr. R. Suresh and Dr. K. Ramesh Kumar for their support in completing the book. We also would like to record our gratitude to Dr. S. Rajendran, Professor of Economics, Gandhigram Rural University, Dindigul, for his constant encouragements in completing the study.

We have immensely benefited from the libraries of the Madras Institute of Development Studies (MIDS), Chennai and the Institute for Social and Economic Change (ISEC), Bangalore. We are thankful to the Librarians of these Institutions. We sincerely hope that the materials presented in the volume will be useful to the students, researchers and policy-makers concerning with irrigation and rural poverty.

Susanto Kumar Beero
Institute of Economic Growth, New Delhi

A. Narayanamoorthy
Alagappa University, Karaikudi, Tamil Nadu

Contents

Acronyms

AA	—	Above Average
AAY	—	Antyodaya Anna Yojana
AED	—	Average Employment Days
AFED	—	Average Farm Employment Days
AIBP	—	Accelerated Irrigation Benefit Programme
ANFED	—	Average Non-Farm Employment Days
ANA	—	Above National Average
AVG	—	Average
AWI	—	Agricultural Wages in India
AWP	—	Agricultural Water Productivity
BA	—	Below Average
BKVY	—	Biju Krushak Vikash Yojana
BNA	—	Below National Average
BPL	—	Below Poverty Line
CAD	—	Command Area Development
CCA	—	Culturable Command Area
CDCP	—	Check Dam Construction Programme
CDP	—	Community Development Programme
CI	—	Cropping Intensity
CIV	—	Canal Irrigated Village
CSRE	—	Cash Scheme for Rural Employment
DBWIP	—	Deep Bore-Well Irrigation Programme
DIASA	—	Districts having Irrigation Above the State Average
DIBSA	—	Districts having Irrigation Below the State Average
DPAP	—	Drought-Prone Areas Programme
DR	—	Dependency Ratio
DRDA	—	District Rural Development Agency
DLP	—	Districts with Lower Poverty
DMP	—	Districts with Medium Poverty
DWCRA	—	Development of Women and Children in Rural Areas

EAS	—	Employment Assurance Scheme
EGS	—	Employment Guarantee Scheme
FAO	—	Food and Agriculture Organization
FGT	—	Foster, Greer, and Thorbecke
FPHRP	—	Foodgrain Production Per Head Rural Population
FS	—	Family Size
FWP	—	Food for Work Programme
GCAPTRP	—	Gross Cropped Area to Per Thousand Rural Population
GDP	—	Gross Domestic Product
GIAGCA	—	Percentage of Gross Irrigated Area to Gross Cropped Area
GIV	—	Groundwater Irrigated Village
GNP	—	Growth National Product
GoI	—	Government of India
GWI	—	Groundwater Irrigation
HA	—	Hectare
HCR	—	Head Count Ratio
HHI	—	Household Industries
HHs	—	Households
HYVP	—	High Yielding Variety Programme
IADP	—	Intensive Agricultural Districts Programme
IAPTRP	—	Irrigated Area Per Thousand Rural Population
ILO	—	International Labour Organization
IRDP	—	Integrated Rural Development Programme
IWMI	—	International Water Management Institute
JGSY	—	Jawahar Gram Samriddhi Yojana
JICA	—	Japan International Co-operation Agency
KM	—	Kilometre
MCP	—	Megalift Construction Programme
MFALDA	—	Marginal Farmers' and Agricultural Labourers' Development Agency
MGNREGS	—	Mahatma Gandhi National Rural Employment Guarantee Scheme
MMRP	—	Modified Mixed Reference Period
MPCE	—	Monthly Per Capita Consumption Expenditure
MPFI	—	Monthly Per Capita Farm Income
MPI	—	Monthly Per Capita Income
MPNFI	—	Monthly Per Capita Non-Farm Income
MRP	—	Mixed Recall Period

NGO	—	Non-Government Organization
NHBPL	—	Number of Households Below Poverty Line
NPBPL	—	Number of Population Below Poverty Line
NREP	—	National Rural Employment Programme
NREGA	—	National Rural Employment Guarantee Scheme
NSS	—	National Sample Survey
NSSO	—	National Sample Survey Organization
OCTMP	—	Odisha Community Tank Management Project
OIIAWMIP	—	Odisha Integrated Irrigated Agriculture and Water Management Investment Programme
OLS	—	Ordinary Least Square
OW	—	Other Workers
PAP	—	Poverty Alleviation Programmes
PFG	—	Productivity of Foodgrain
PFWTWI	—	Percentage of Farm Wage to Total Wage Income
PHBPL	—	Percentage of Household Below Poverty Line
PIREP	—	Pilot Intensive Rural Employment Project
PNFWTWI	—	Percentage of Non-Farm Wage to Total Wage Income
PPBPL	—	Percentage of Population Below Poverty Line
PRISM	—	Poverty Reduction through Irrigation and Smallholder Markets
PPP	—	Purchasing Power Parity
PRP	—	Percentage of Rural Poverty
REL	—	Rural Labour Enquiries
RFV	—	Rainfed Village
RIDF	—	Rural Infrastructure Development Fund
RLEGP	—	Rural Landless Employment Guarantee Programme
RRR	—	Repair, Renovation, Restoration of Water Bodies
RWAL	—	Real Wage Rate of Agriculture Labourer
SC	—	Scheduled Caste
SD	—	Standard Deviation
SDPAHRP	—	State Domestic Product of Agriculture Per Head Rural Population
SFDA	—	Small Farmers Development Agency
SGRY	—	Sampurna Gramin Rojgar Yojana
SGSY	—	Swarnajayanti Gram Swarozgar Yojana
ST	—	Scheduled Tribe
TIV	—	Tank Irrigated Village

TPP	—	Twenty Point Programme
TRYSEM	—	Training of Rural Youth for Self-Employment
WRAL	—	Wage Rate of Agricultural Labourer
UNDP	—	United Nation Development Programme
URP	—	Uniform Recall Period
VAO	—	Village Administrative Officer
WPR	—	Work Participation Rate

List of Tables

List of Maps and Figures

List of Maps

List of Figures

1
Introduction

1.1. Preamble

India is the second most populous country in the world, with 1.21 billion people living in 640 districts of 29 States and seven Union Territories. The population of India is represented by 17.5 per cent of the world's population, which is more than a sixth of the world's population (Census of India, 2011). The total area of the country is 32,87,263 sq. kms, which is 2.42 per cent of world area, having occupied seventh place in the world. The net area under cultivation is about 142 million hectares, out of which 125 million hectares (75.75% of net sown area) are under foodgrain cultivation. The net irrigated area was about 45 per cent of the cropped area in 2012-13 (GoI, 2014).

Poverty remains a persistent feature in India despite over a century of debate, action and aid to transform the livelihoods of the poor. The poverty is multidimensional concept, extending from low levels of income and consumption to lack of education and malnutrition. As pointed out by Tendulkar Committee (Planning Commission, 2013), the concept of poverty is associated with socially perceived deprivation with respect to basic human needs. But, due to variation of basic needs across time and space, the poverty lines also vary depending upon the level of socio-economic development, social norms and values within regions in a country or cross-countries (Hussain *et al.*, 2006). Therefore, the Planning Commission is periodically revising the poverty line to measure the poverty ratio of India, from time to time.

As known to all, calorie concept is the measuring rod of poverty. The first Director General of FAO (Food and Agricultural Organisation) was the first person to propound the starvation line, in

1945, which referred to the consumption of less than 2300 calories per person per day. This idea explained the poverty line. By adopting this idea, Planning Commission of India also defined poverty line on the basis of recommended nutritional requirements of 2400 calories per person per day for rural areas and 2100 calories per person per day for urban areas. Based on this nutritional criterion, the income criterion has been adopted in India to determine the poverty line. The latest criterion to determine poverty line in India is based on 2011-12 data, where it is stated that all-India level minimum income of rural and urban areas, for a person per month, should be Rs. 816.00 and Rs. 1000.00 respectively (see, Table 1.1).

Table 1.1: Trends in Poverty Ratio and Poverty Line in India

Years	*Poverty Ratio (%)*			*Poverty Line (Rs.)*	
	Rural	*Urban*	*Total*	*Rural*	*Urban*
1973-74	56.44	49.09	54.88	49.63	56.64
1977-78	53.07	45.24	51.32	56.84	72.50
1983	45.65	40.79	44.49	89.50	115.65
1987-88	39.09	38.20	38.86	115.43	165.58
1993-94	37.27	32.26	35.97	205.84	281.35
1999-2000	27.09	23.62	26.10	327.56	454.11
2004-05	28.30	25.70	27.50	446.68	578.80
2011-12	25.70	13.70	21.92	816.00	1000.00

Source: Government of India (2014).

Before 2004-05, population under poverty was estimated in India mainly based on expenditure on food items, but the United Nations Development Programme (UNDP), in their 1990 report, specifically mentioned that minimum income does not lead to basic survival needs and for standard of living. For the first time, Uniform Recall Period (URP) and Mixed Recall Period (MRP) concepts were used in 2004-05 to determine below poverty line population in India. The URP and MRP are based on consumer expenditure data both for food and non-food items. In the case of URP, consumer expenditure data, for all items, were collected from a 30-day recall period. On the other hand, MRP data throw light on food and non-food items. For MRP, consumer expenditure data for five non-food items, namely clothing, footwear, durable goods, education and institutional medical expenses were collected from 365-day recall period and the consumption data for the remaining items were collected from 30-day recall period. The National Sample Survey Organisation (NSSO) tabulated expenditure details of about 1.20 lakh households. Since these households reported different number of members, the NSSO, for the purpose of comparison, divided the household expenditure by the number of members in a household to arrive at per capita consumption expenditure per month. Thus, Monthly Per Capita Consumption Expenditure (MPCE) is computed on the basis of three different concepts: (i) Uniform Reference Period (URP); (ii) Mixed Reference Period (MRP), and (iii) Modified Mixed Reference Period (MMRP). As per the Tendulkar Methodology (Planning Commission, 2013), the poverty line has been expressed in terms of MPCE, based on Mixed Reference Period (see, Table 1.1).

Presently, according to the Tendulkar Methodology (Planning Commission, 2013), poverty line has been fixed based on MPCE. While the overall poverty rate in India was 54.88 per cent in 1973-74, the poverty rate in urban and rural areas were 49.09 per cent and 56.44 per cent respectively during the same period. There was consistent reduction in poverty rate from 1973-74 to 1999-2000. The poverty rate declined in India from 54.88 per cent in 1973-74 to 26.10 per cent in the year 1999-2000. Urban and Rural poverty rate declined from 49.09 per cent and 56.44 per cent to 23.62 per cent and 27.09 per cent respectively in the year 1999-2000 (see, Table 1.1). Thereafter, poverty continued to increase throughout the 1990s and went up to 27.50, 25.70 and 28.30 per cent for all-India, urban and rural respectively in 2004-05. Again poverty rate started declining from 2004-05 to 2011-12.

The levels of poverty were somewhat higher in the rural areas relative to those in urban and overall poverty in the country. This is because the rural poverty is determined by the agricultural growth. However, the present situation in agricultural growth is erratic. There is evidence from many developing countries that increasing agricultural productivity is a key to poverty reduction. High economic growth, increased income and improved nutrition have been linked to improvements in rural and agricultural development in many countries in Asia between 1970 and 1990. On the other hand, several countries in Africa experienced that real decline in agricultural growth negatively impacted the national Gross National Product (GNP) and increased poverty level (Coxhead and Warr, 1995). The performance of agricultural sector influences the growth of Indian Economy. Agricultural has been a way of life and the most important livelihood to the masses.

Achieving minimum agricultural growth is a prerequisite for inclusive growth, reduction of poverty levels, development of the rural economy and enhancing of farm income. Agricultural growth basically depends on agricultural major factor inputs such as irrigation, cropped area, labour, fertilizer etc. Among the major factor inputs, irrigation is an important factor for agricultural development. Increase in agricultural production and productivity depend, to a large extent, on the availability of water. Irrigation access has strong poverty-reduction impact by enhancing productivity and increasing cropping intensity, making more profitable cropping patterns accessible to small holders, offering more employment opportunities at a higher wage rate to the agricultural labourers, and increasing income and purchasing power of the agricultural wage labourers (Narayanamoorthy, 2001; Shah and Singh, 2004).

Irrigation water has been regarded as a powerful factor for providing food security, rural and agricultural development, economic growth, famine protection, land use intensification, protection against adverse drought conditions, increased prospects for employment and stable income, and greater opportunity for multiple cropping and crop diversification (Husain *et al.*, 2002). There is also a positive impact of irrigation on real wages of agricultural labourers (Narayanamoorthy and Despande, 2003).

Realizing the importance of irrigation, the Government of India has been making enormous efforts for irrigation development from the initiation of planning in India. At the beginning of the planning (1950-51), irrigation schemes were divided into three categories; major, medium and minor. Major irrigation costs more than Rs. 5 crore each, medium irrigation costs between Rs. 10 lakh and Rs. 5 crore each and minor irrigation costs less than Rs. 10 lakh. This scheme continued till 1978 and then the new classification was adopted in April 1978. The new schemes are: (i) major schemes are defined as those having Culturable Command Area (CCA) of more than 10,000 hectares, (ii) medium schemes as those having CCA between 2,000 hectares and 10,000 hectares, and (iii) minor scheme as those having CCA of less than 2,000 hectares.

As mentioned above, starting from the First Five Year Plan period, huge investments have been made for the development of irrigation infrastructure in India. The irrigation investment rose to Rs. 36,649 crore in the Eight Five Year Plan from Rs. 442 crore in the First Five Year Plan. The outlay for irrigation and flood control in the Ninth

Five Year Plan was Rs. 63,682 crores. Of this, Rs. 48,259 crores (76%) was for major and medium irrigation projects and the balance Rs. 15,423 crore (24%) for minor irrigation Command Area Development (CAD) programme and flood control. The outlay on irrigation and flood control in the Tenth Five Year Plan (2002-07) was kept at Rs. 95,743 crore. Total outlay for irrigation in the Eleventh Plan (2007-12) was kept at Rs. 2,32,311 crore (at 2004-05 prices). Substantial expenditure has gone in for developing the major and medium irrigation potential, especially the major river valley projects like the Bhakra-Nangal Project (Punjab), Beas Project (Punjab and Haryana), Hirakud Dam Project (Odisha), Damodar Valley Corporation (Bihar and West Bengal), Nagarjunasagar Project (Andhra Pradesh and Karnataka), etc.

For the purpose of irrigation development, presently, the following programmes are being implemented by the Government of India. These programmes are: Accelerated Irrigation Benefit Programme (AIBP), Rural Infrastructure Development Fund (RIDF), Biju Krishak Vikash Yojana (BKVY), Japan International Co-operation Agency (JICA), Odisha Integrated Irrigated Agriculture and Water Management Investment Programme (OIIAWMIP), Odisha Community Tank Management Project (OCTMP), Dam Rehabilitation and Improvement Project (DRIP), Check Dam Construction Programme (CDCP), Deep Bore-Well Irrigation Programme (DBWIP), Repair, Renovation, Restoration of water bodies (RRR) and Megalift Construction Programme (MCP). As a result of concerted effort taken by the government, the irrigated area of the country has increased from 22.56 million hectares in 1950-51 to over 92 million hectares in 2012-13 (GoI, 2014).

The massive investment on irrigation, during the planning periods, has not only increased agricultural production but also greatly improved the income of the farmers, employment opportunity for agricultural labourers and benefited the entire population by providing more food at lower prices (Thorat and Fan, 2007). However, irrigation systems completely depend on rainfall. If there is monsoon failure, no water can be gathered in tank/small water body for irrigation purpose. There will be scarcity of ground water for pumping out because the water level in the ground will go down and excess exploitation of water from the ground will cause land degradation and environmental hazards and then there will be no water in river basins for canal irrigation. Due to low level of rainfall, the sufficiency of irrigation comes down as well.

Irrigation significantly can help to increase agricultural production and productivity. However, the availability of irrigation facility is highly inadequate in India. For example, in 1950-51, gross irrigated area as percentage of gross cropped area was only 17 per cent. Despite massive investments on irrigation projects over the periods of planning, gross irrigated area as percentage of gross cropped area was only about 45 percentage in 2013-14. Thus, even now more than 55 per cent of the gross cropped area depends on rain. That is why Indian agriculture is called "a gamble in the monsoons".

Access to reliable irrigation facility enables farmers to adopt new technologies and intensify cultivation. This facilitates increased productivity and overall higher production, and greater returns from farming, increase in their production and income, enhancing opportunities to diversify their income base, reducing vulnerability caused by the seasonality of agricultural production as well as external shocks (Narayanamoorthy, 2001). This, in turn, opens up new employment opportunities, both on-farm and off-farm, and can improve income, livelihoods, and the quality of life in rural areas. Thus, access to good irrigation has the potential to contribute to poverty reduction and the movement of people from ill-being to well-being (Husain *et al.*, 2002). However, there are vast areas, with established irrigation systems, where productivity and incomes of farmers remained low due to various reasons (Hussain and Hanjra, 2003). The entrenched pockets of poverty persist in many States. The effects of these changes on the efficiency and equity of water use are not yet clear, especially with regard to poverty. Though the importance of irrigation in agricultural development is well recognised by several studies, irrigation-poverty linkages have not been studied in a greater depth. In this study, therefore, an attempt has been made to fill this gap.

1.2. Problem Specification

India, like many other developing countries, has primarily been an agricultural country. Agriculture in India is the lifeblood of the nation. Agriculture is the largest sector of the economic activity and plays a crucial role in the country's economic development by providing food and raw materials to industrial sectors and employment to a large proportion of the population. Thus, improvement in the agricultural sector has a far reaching impact on the overall growth of the country's Gross Domestic Product (GDP). Its importance is clear from its contribution of 14 per cent to GDP, 58 per cent to the total labour force and 38 per cent foreign exchange earnings (GoI, 2013). Due to hard working manpower and large irrigation systems and its rich land resources, India has the obvious comparative advantage in the development of its agriculture which would change the fate of the majority of the people of the rural areas.

Agriculture not only provides food and employment to the people, raw material to most industries and earns foreign exchange, but also plays a leading role in eradicating poverty in the less developed countries. In a shrinking world, poverty has become an international priority and a moral imperative (Bravo, 2002). Ravallion and Datt (1997), in their study, stated that poverty reduction in India is the result of growth in crop yields and not the transfer of poor from agriculture to off-farm sector or industrial growth. They also showed that agricultural sector growth had significant poverty reduction in India. Timmer (1997) showed this to be true for 35 countries covered by his analysis and concluded that growth in agricultural output results to increase the income of the agricultural labourers and farmers. Thus, the increase and decrease of rural poverty depend upon the growth of agriculture (Ahluwalia, 1978; Mellor, 1985). Agriculture sector, in developing countries like India, is widely considered to play a vital role in the eradication of poverty. Therefore, poverty is not only an effect but also a cause of low agricultural productivity (Ahmad, 2003). Agricultural production, based on modern technology, requires all round institutional and infrastructural support. As stated earlier, agricultural growth takes place due to increased use of agricultural inputs: high-yielding variety seeds, fertilizer, irrigation, cropped area, labour, good organisation, technological change etc. (Reddy, 1995; Narayanamoorthy, 2001; Dethier and Effenberger, 2011). Among various agricultural inputs, water is an important prerequisite for agricultural development (Reddy, 1995).

Increase in agricultural production and productivity depend, to a large extent, on availability of water. Irrigated area constitutes not only about 45 per cent of the total cultivated area but also contributes to almost 60 per cent of the food grains production in the country. This shows that irrigation contributes towards agricultural output. In fact, the target of doubling foodgrain production, in the next 10 years, would mainly depend the availability, performance and efficiency of irrigation. For the efficient performance of irrigation, the three major sources of irrigation (tank irrigation, canal irrigation and groundwater irrigation) have given birth to so many types of irrigation system like drip irrigation, sprinkler irrigation, soaker hose, ditch irrigation, terraced irrigation, rotary irrigation system, centre pivot irrigation, etc. These new and different types of irrigation systems are very useful for production of different types of crop year-round. By this new system of irrigation, huge amount of water can be saved from wastage, can be used efficiently and resourcefully and then increased cropping intensity, multiple cropping system, year-round cultivation and increased productivity can be attained from the scanty water irrigation.

The East India Company (ECI) servant, Sir Charles Trevelyan, noted in 1816 that "irrigation is everything in India; water is more valuable than land, because when water is applied to land it increases its productiveness at least six-fold and renders great extents of land productive, which otherwise would produce nothing or next to nothing" (quoted by Sharma, 2002). Moreover, Knowels, in 1948, observed that irrigation works provided security in life, increased the yields and the value of the land and the revenue derived from it. They have lessened the cost of famine relief and have helped to civilise the whole region.

In an agrarian economy like India, irrigation may be a good source of employment as well. Irrigation raises both employment and income level of land and thus adds to capital formation. Irrigation has a considerable impact on the social and economic life of the people not only living within the command area but also outside the command area (Reddy, 1995). The growth of the agricultural sector, aided by irrigation development, has broad impact on the poverty alleviation of the people of the rural areas (Dev, 1988; Fan *et al.*, 1999; Mellor, 2001; Narayanamoorthy, 2001). In addition, the irrigation benefits are more to the population living in the low income quintile as compared to the upper income quintile because irrigation generates employment and other feed backs in the rural economies. Bhattarai and Narayanamoorthy (2003), in their analysis, demonstrated that among all the variables selected for analysing the poverty measures, irrigation has a crucial role in the reduction of poverty. Compared with rural literacy, irrigation has a much bigger marginal impact on the poverty reduction.

Irrigation water contributes to many productive and livelihood activities. Irrigation water is linked to poverty alleviation, both directly and indirectly. Direct linkages of irrigation and poverty are through localised and household level. Indirect linkages of irrigation and poverty are regional, national and economy-wide growth level. Irrigation can benefit the poor through raising yields and production, lowering the risk of crop failure, and generating higher and year-round farm and non-farm employment (Narayanamoorthy, 2001, 2007; Bhattarai and Narayanamoorthy, 2003). It enables small-holders to adopt more diversified cropping pattern and to switch from low-value subsistence production to high-value, market-oriented production.

Irrigation investments act as production and supply shifters and they have a strong positive effect on growth, benefiting population in the long run. Further, irrigation benefits also accrue to the poor and landless in the long run, although in the short run, relative benefits to the landless and land-poor may be small, as the allocation of water often tends to be land-based. In spite of this, the poor and the landless also benefit from irrigation investments through increased food supplies and lower food prices. To sum up, irrigation can influence poverty through three pathways: (a) micro-pathway or productivity pathway; (b) mesopathway or market participation pathway; and (c) macro-pathway or growth pathway (Hussain, 2004). Therefore, Narayanamoorthy (2001), in his study, stated that irrigation reduces rural poverty by increasing employment days and then income of agricultural labour households and by enhancing availability of food with affordable prices. The intensive cultivation of crops, due to timely access to groundwater irrigation, increases the demand for agricultural labourers and hence wages rate for those who are mostly living below poverty line in India (Narayanamoorthy and Deshpande, 2003).

As stated earlier, there are mainly three types of irrigation sources, namely, well/groundwater irrigation, canal irrigation and tank irrigation, available in India. Of these three, groundwater irrigation has become a dominant source of irrigation in Indian agriculture in terms of reliability, timely availability and controllability. The timely availability of groundwater irrigation helps to increase the cropping intensity, productivity and production of crops, allows the farmers to shift the cropping pattern from low-value to high-value crops, and then it increases the demand for agricultural labourers and enhances wage rates for those who mostly live below the poverty line (Vaidyanathan, 1996). The development of groundwater irrigation also benefits the non-tube-well-owning small farmers through the water market (Shah,

1993; Narayanamoorthy, 1994, 1996). Both increased affordability of food grains and increased wage rates have substantially reduced poverty in areas where groundwater irrigation is well developed. Thus, groundwater irrigation is very crucial for the farmers as well as the agricultural labourers to cross the poverty line.

If irrigation has the potential to produce such profound impact on rural poverty alleviation, why such impact is not visible in India where it is greatly needed and has the water resources to sustain intensive irrigation (Shah and Singh, 2004). There are several studies regarding irrigation and agricultural development in India. There are also studies available about the role of agriculture on income, employment opportunity and rural poverty alleviation. A few relevant studies have also analysed the importance of irrigation on rural poverty. But there are no studies available on the nexus between irrigation development and rural poverty covering various States in India from 1973-74 to 2011-12. And also studies are absolutely not available, using primary and secondary data in India, on the nexus between irrigation and rural poverty. Keeping this in view, an attempt has been made in this study to test the relationship between the incidence of rural poverty and the development of irrigation using both macro and micro-level data in India.

1.3. Justification of the Study

The core focus of this study is to understand the linkages between irrigation development and rural poverty. Though there are studies which do point out that increased irrigation development can reduce rural poverty, directly or indirectly, there are gaps in the available studies on irrigation development and poverty alleviation. Although irrigation has been recognised as a crucial factor in explaining the growth in agriculture and rural economy in the literature, it has not been related with the rural poverty. The explanation of cross-section variations in rural poverty has all along been sought through agricultural growth (Ahluwalia, 1978), average value of agricultural output per hectare (Sundaram and Tendulkar, 1988) or through output per hectare (Datt and Ravallion, 1996; Ravallion and Datt, 1996). However, the use of irrigation as an explanatory variable had not been attempted by studies on rural poverty till the year 2001. After the publication of Narayanamoorthy (2001), quite a few studies have attempted to study the nexus between the irrigation development and rural poverty, by using aggregated and disaggregated data in India and in South Asia (Bhattarai and Narayanamoorthy, 2003; Saleth *et al.*, 2003; Hussain and Hanjra, 2003, 2004; Shah and Singh, 2004; Hussain, 2007c; Lipton, 2007; Narayanamoorthy, 2007; Narayanamoorthy and Hanjra, 2010). It is well recognised by these studies that irrigation is one of the principal causative factors, behind the temporal changes in agricultural growth and hence directly using irrigation as an explanatory factor is necessary.

The available studies on the irrigation-poverty nexus have certain limitations. First, the variable of irrigation has not been properly defined and used in the analysis and in most cases percentage of irrigated area to cropped area is used for the analysis, which does not capture the density of irrigation in relation to rural population. Second, irrigation has not been used as a lagged variable in the regression analysis, which is needed because irrigation cannot instantaneously impact the rural poverty. Third, most studies have used very old data, covering the period only up to 1993-94, which does not capture the current reality. Fourth, studies covering all the major States, with all the eight time points of poverty data from 1973-74 to 2011-12, are seldom available. Fifth, there are no studies available on the nexus between irrigation development and rural poverty for the study period 1973-74 till date covering various districts in India. Sixth, studies are not available, using primary data in India, on the issue of irrigation and rural poverty nexus. Keeping this in view, an attempt has been made in this study to test the relationship between the incidence of rural poverty and the development of irrigation using both macro and micro-level data from India.

1.4. Objectives

The main objectives of the study are:

1. To study the relationship between irrigation development and the rural poverty across the major States in India, from 1973-74 to 2011-12.
2. To analyse the impact of irrigation on rural poverty across the districts in India.
3. To study the relationship between base level irrigation and rural poverty.
4. To analyse the impact of source-wise irrigation on rural poverty utilising the field survey data.

1.5. Chapter Scheme

This study is organised into eight chapters. The introduction part, on the issue of irrigation and rural poverty nexus, is dealt with in the first chapter. The second chapter presents the relevant literature at length. The details of the methodological part are illustrated in chapter three. The fourth chapter presents the general description of the study area. The fifth chapter describes the impact of irrigation on rural poverty across States in India. District-level analysis on poverty and irrigation nexus is dealt with the sixth chapter. Seventh chapter presents the analysis on the source-wise irrigation impact on rural poverty from the field survey data. The last chapter provides the major findings of the study along with suggestions.

2
Review of Literature

2.1. Introduction

There are various studies in India and in other countries of the world on the issue of irrigation and poverty alleviation. Among the extant studies, the most relevant studies are selected and reviewed in this chapter. These studies are discussed in six different sections. The first section reviews the role of Government policy on poverty reduction. The importance of irrigation on agricultural productivity, employment and income are discussed in the second section. The third section deals with agricultural productivity, wage income and poverty. Agriculture and rural poverty reduction is discussed in the fourth section. Section five is based on source-wise impact of irrigation on rural poverty. While the section six focuses on the impact of irrigation on rural poverty alleviation, the concluding remark on literature is presented in section seven.

2.2. Role of Government Policy in Poverty Reduction

Poverty has been the primary issue in India. The Government has come out with numerous plans and policies for the eradication of poverty in rural areas. Quite a few relevant studies (Rao, 1978; Sundaram and Tendulkar, 1988; Rath, 1985; Rao, 1987, 1992; Kumar, 1993) are available focusing on the role of Government in poverty reduction. After the adoption of the new Constitution by the Constituent Assembly of India early in 1950, the Government of India established the Planning Commission to appraise the country's material, capital and human resources and to formulate a plan for their effective and balanced utilisation.

The major objectives of economic planning in India are: (1) rapid economic growth, (2) removal of poverty and unemployment, (3) reduction of economic inequalities, (4) self-reliance, (5) balanced regional development, and (6) employment generation. In one way or the other, these major objectives of economic planning focused on reducing poverty in India.

On the issue of poverty alleviation, rural development and rural employment programmes were first adopted in the 1970s. Poverty alleviation came to be accepted as one of the principle objectives of economic planning in India. During the Fifth Five Year Plan, a number of poverty alleviation programmes were introduced. Of these, the important schemes were: Small Farmers Development Agency (SFDA), Marginal Farmers' and Agricultural Labourers' Development Agency (MFALDA), Drought-Prone Areas Programme (DPAP), Cash Scheme for Rural Employment (CSRE), Pilot Intensive Rural Employment Project (PIREP) and Food for Work Programme (FWP).

At the outset, the Community Development Programme (CDP) (1951) was introduced in the First Five Year Plan (1951-56) for overall development of rural areas. Secondly, High Yielding Variety Programme (HYVP) was introduced (1966-67) to increase productivity of food grains, which is the major component to reduce poverty, by adopting latest varieties of inputs for crops. Also Green Revolution was introduced to increase the food grains, especially wheat production during this period.

During the Fourth Five Year Plan (1969-74), Cash Scheme for Rural Employment (CSRE) was established in 1972-73 to enhance employment opportunities for rural people because employment opportunities for rural people had direct impact on rural poverty alleviation. The Twenty-Point Programme (TPP) was announced (in 1975) for poverty eradication and raising the standard of living during the Fifth Five Year Plan (1974-79).

Though various development and employment programmes, directly or indirectly, contributed to poverty reduction, poverty alleviation became the core objective of Sixth Five Year Plan (1980-85). The progressive reduction in poverty and generation of employment were accorded very high priority in the Seventh Five Year Plan (1985-90), Eighth Five Year Plan (1997-2002), Tenth Five Year Plan (2002-07) and Eleventh Five Year Plan (2007-12). Even the Twelfth Five Year Plan was concerned with 'Poverty alleviation' as the main objective.

The Integrated Rural Development Programme (IRDP) was launched during 1980 (during the Sixth Five Year Plan) for all-round development of rural poor through a programme of asset endowment for self-employment. The National Rural Employment Programme (NREP) was introduced in the year 1980 for providing profitable employment opportunities to the rural areas during this period. Development of Women and Children in Rural Areas (DWCRA) commenced in September 1982, to provide suitable opportunities of self-employment to women belonging to the rural families who are living below the poverty line during this plan. Also, Rural Landless Employment Guarantee Programme (RLEGP) was initiated in the month of August 15, 1983 to provide employment to landless farmers and labourers during this period. Further, Integrated Rural Development Programme (IRDP), National Rural Employment Programme (NREP) and Rural Landless Employment Guarantee Programme (RLEGP) were created with the objective of poverty alleviation.

During the Eighth Five Year Plan (1992-97), the Employment Assurance Scheme (EAS) was introduced in October 2, 1993 to provide employment for at least 100 days in a year in villages and to alleviate rural poverty. The District Rural Development Agency (DRDA) was launched in 1993 to provide financial assistance for rural development in this period. Also, National Social Assistance Programme (1995) was instituted to assist people living below the poverty line.

Swarna Jayanti Gram Swarozgar Yojana (SJGSY) was introduced in April 1999 for eliminating rural poverty, unemployment and promoting self-employment. Jawahar Gram Samriddhi Yojana (JGSY) proposed in April 1999 to create demand driven community village infrastructure. Antyodaya Anna Yojana (AAY) was formed on December 25, 2000 for providing food security to poor, Sampurna Gramin Rojgar Yojana (SGRY) was launched in September 25, 2001, to provide employment and food security and Jai Prakash Narain Rojgar Guarantee (JPNRG) (2002) to ensure employment guarantee in most of the poor districts in India during the Ninth Five Year Plan.

Bharat Nirman Programme (BNP) was launched on December 16, 2005, for the development of rural infrastructure which included six components: irrigation, water supply, housing, road, telephone and electricity, during the Tenth Five Year Plan (2002-07). These six components were designed for reducing rural poverty. Another important programme of National Rural Employment Guarantee Scheme (NREGS) was initiated during this plan period (February 2, 2006) to provide at least 100 days wage employment in rural areas.

The Planning Commission has been estimating the incidence of poverty at the National and State-level by using the methodology proposed by the Lakdawala Committee. The poverty was estimated, based on consumption expenditure data, from the large sample surveys on consumer expenditure, conducted by the NSSO at an interval of approximately five years. Later, in view of controversy around the measurement of poverty and other unresolved issues, the Planning Commission of India constituted an expert group called the Tendulkar Committee in December 2005, to review the methodology for estimation of poverty.

Widespread poverty in India has attracted the attention of a number of economists and organisations. Leading studies in poverty have been conducted by Dandekar and Rath, B.S. Minhas, P.K. Bardhan, World Bank and the Planning Commission of India. In their book, on "Poverty in India" (1971), Dandekar and Rath made a path-breaking study of the poverty phenomenon in India. Using the National Sample Survey (NSS) data on consumption, they concluded that in 1960-61, about 40 per cent of urban population and about 50 per cent of rural population lived below the poverty line.

For the first time in the history of Indian planning, Rao (1973) studied the objective of Fifth Five Year Plan. The objective of Fifth Five Year Plan was to provide minimum consumption for the bottom 30 per cent of the population. In this study, he stated that to realise this objective, there has to be two sides (demand and supply side). On the supply side, the volume and composition of output, consistent with these consumption targets, have to be planned for. On the demand side, the plan investments have to be such that they generate the required income for the poor. He explored how much income needs to be generated for the poor if the minimum consumption objective is to be achieved according to the Fifth Five Year Plan.

Similarly, progressive reduction in the incidence of poverty was one of the major objectives of the Sixth Five Year Plan. Sundaram and Tendulkar (1983) made an attempt to evaluate the trends in poverty during the Plan. They explored that there was progressive reduction in the incidence of poverty in the Sixth Five Year Plan. The population below the poverty line was 48.14 per cent in 1979-80, but 30 per cent in 1984-85. It meant that there was a reduction in the number of poor from about 317 million in 1979-80 to 215 million people in the terminal year of the Plan.

Since the problem of rural poverty is old and massive in India, the main objective of Integrated Rural Development Programme (IRDP) is to have all-round development of rural poor through a programme of asset endowment for self-employment. Rath (1985), in his study, examined whether IRDP reduced rural poverty. The results of the analysis showed that IRDP had reduced rural poverty by providing cattle, other assets and subsidy to the farmers and more employment opportunities to the rural poor. The study suggested that eradication of poverty demanded a multipronged strategy, including the IRDP.

In the other study, Rao (1987) investigated small farmers, marginal farmers and agricultural labour households which exercised impact on rural poverty. The study was carried out in four villages of Gujarat in 1980-81, the year when IRDP was launched. The method of data collection was through structured questionnaires. Over all, the findings of the study were that rural poverty was reduced due to irrigation, improved tools and extension of new technology undertaken by public body through various rural development programmes. The author suggested reducing the dependence of the poor on the rural rich (1) by providing consumption credit; (2) by allocating funds, on the basis of micro-level planning, taking into account the resource potential of the area, the incidence of unemployment, the nature and extent of poverty etc.; and (3) by encouraging the poorest of the poor to take up wage employment.

Rao (1992) again made an attempt to examine the potential as well as the prospects for integrating the major Poverty Alleviation Programmes (PAPs). The study stated that the potential for such integration was quite high, both by way of better choice of activities and more effective implementation of the activities chosen. It further stated that three major initiatives were taken by the Government during the Sixth and Seventh Five Year Plans for self-employment and to increase income of the poor. They were: Integrated Rural Development Programme (IRDP), Training of Rural Youth for Self-Employment (TRYSEM) and Development of Women and Children in Rural Areas (DWCRA).

Based on the above study, Kumar (1993) evaluated the measurement of poverty alleviation programmes. This study analysed by taking into account the income distribution of head count ratio and using cumulative distribution function. The study recorded that using the rate of change of head count ratio to evaluate the performance of poverty alleviation was biased against those States or regions which were poorer, to start with. The study noted four measures of poverty and they were: (i) the head count ratio (H), (ii) the income gap ratio (I), (iii) Sen's index of poverty (P), and (iv) Foster, Greer, and Thorbecke (FGT) index (P). The author suggested that in order to evaluate the performance of poverty alleviation programme, the four methods to follow were: (a) identification of the poor; (b) identification of different degrees of poverty; (c) distribution of households according to different degrees of poverty; and (d) the identification of policy-makers attached to different degrees of poverty.

In another study, Parthasarathy (1995) evaluated public intervention programmes for the rural poor against the background of the socio-economic context, trends in growth and rural poverty in Andhra Pradesh. The author stated that such a performance was understandable for the 1970s, during which period agricultural growth in Andhra Pradesh was high, but was confusing, particularly in the latter part of 1980s during which period agricultural growth performance had considerably slackened. Such developments were significant to an examination of the role of public intervention and its implications for a sustainable reduction of poverty.

Further, Sagar (1995) examined the role of public intervention in poverty alleviation in Rajasthan. Secondary data of household income, agricultural labourers, crop groups and drought pattern in Rajasthan, were used for the study. The author found that in spite of fluctuating levels of rainfall, low levels of agricultural production, unemployment situation, regional variations in poverty levels and very low level of economic and social development, there was a positive record of achievements in poverty alleviation. The study suggested that an emphasis on infrastructural development, especially watershed development and reforestation, along with programmes of employment and asset redistribution, were very much crucial for the poverty alleviation.

Bhalla (1995) reviewed the policy for poverty alleviation and rural development in Haryana State. The study found that the poverty ratio was declining continuously over the last 25 years to the point where the State now recorded the second lowest incidence of poverty in the country. But, the process of public intervention, through

Centrally-sponsored programmes for poverty alleviation, was strictly peripheral. Though the strategy of investment in rural infrastructure, agriculture and industrial development had worked, Haryana was still poor regarding the quality of life indicators such as health, mortality and sex-ratio. The author suggested that sustained growth in agriculture plus a deliberate policy of income and occupational diversification are the most effective cure for poverty.

Vyas and Bhargava (1995) also analysed the role of public intervention for poverty alleviation. Nine States were selected for an in-depth study. The study maintained that although there was a high degree of uniformity in the approach and content of poverty alleviation programmes (PAPs) in India, there is a great variation across States in the outcome of these programmes. To conclude, the experience of several Indian States suggested that if the strategies for poverty alleviation are properly planned and implemented, even without spectacular economic growth or a major overhaul of the institutions and structures, the poverty ratio among rural households could be brought down to a tolerable limit.

In another study, Shergill and Singh (1995) examined the trend in rural poverty in Punjab, by analysing the time series data, spanning 1963-64 to 1990-91. The authors widely asserted that there was significant decline in poverty in Punjab due to impressive agricultural growth in the last three decades (Green Revolution Decades) from 1960-61 to 1990-91. Further, the analysis showed that there was a decline not only in the proportion of the poor but also the absolute numbers of the poor and ultra poor due to the green revolution.

Tendulkar and Jain (1995) studied the impact of economic reforms since 1991 on poverty. Having taken the evidence from the National Sample Surveys conducted during 1991 (July-December) and 1992 (January-December), they analysed the factors governing rural and urban poverty. The authors revealed that the economic reforms contributed indirectly to sharp reduction of rural poverty during the period under consideration.

Chaudhuri and Gupta (1995), in their study, made an attempt to map poverty in the districts of Indian States to examine their spatial disparity within and across the States. The study used the consumer expenditure data from the National Sample Survey Organisation for 2004-05. The sample design covered districts as strata, in both the rural and urban sectors. The study concluded that there was variation in poverty ratio in the districts of the country due to social, political and economical constraints. Importantly, unequal performance of poverty alleviation programmes is the cause for variation in poverty in the districts of the States.

Sharma (1995) reviewed the political economy of poverty in Bihar. The author stated that though natural or technological factors such as floods, poor development of infrastructure and high population density were mainly responsible for high incidence of poverty, the State's backwardness was related more to the iniquitous and exploitative socio-economic structure. Though, the poverty alleviation programme and agricultural labourers' movement improved the lot of the poor, execution of poverty alleviation programmes was limited. It is clear from the study that poverty alleviation programme had little impact on alleviating rural poverty in Bihar.

Ravallion and Datt (1996), in their study, analysed the trend in poverty reduction rate data for 40 years. The study revealed that the progress against poverty in India was highly uneven over time and space and trend rates of poverty reduction differed appreciably between States. The higher growth rates in agriculture yields and real non-agricultural output per capita, lower rates of inflation and higher growth in State development expenditure, all led to higher rates of progress, in both raising average consumption and reducing all three measures of absolute poverty. The results also pointed out that higher initial irrigation intensity, higher literacy rates and lower initial infant mortality rates had contributed to higher rates of consumption growth and poverty reduction.

In another study, the poverty alleviation programme, after the post-liberalisation period, in the tribal block in Odisha, was examined by Samal (1998). The study pointed out that the chronic poverty and hunger remained serious problems in spite of economic growth. India implemented various poverty alleviation programmes like other developing countries. But the author suggested that besides these programmes, empowerment through local democracy, land reform and education, investment in irrigation and proper system of credit delivery, steps for the growth of rural non-farm sector and organisation of rural poor are essential to empower the rural poor which can alleviate poverty and eradicate hunger.

Desai and Namboodiri (1998) studied the policy strategy and the instrument for rural poverty alleviation. The crucial objectives of this study were: government policy regarding target-group, government expenditure for agricultural growth and poverty alleviation programmes. After taking Head Count Ratio (HCR), the study maintained that agricultural growth and absolute rural poverty were compatible and well acclaimed for a country where the fortunes of poor were intimately linked to agricultural performance. The strategy for technology-led agricultural growth was more potent than either poverty alleviation programmes or land redistribution measures in alleviating absolute rural poverty. The impact of agricultural performance on absolute poverty was linked to current ramification of farm employment and income.

Similarly, Bardhan and Mookherjee (2004) took a sample of 89 villages of four successive Panchayat administrations and tried to analyse the poverty alleviation efforts of West Bengal Panchayats, implementation of land reforms and pro-poor targeting of credit, agricultural minikits, employment programmes and fiscal grants. The study revealed that the efforts of poverty alleviation were high and there were significant variations both across and within villages over time. They again suggested that poverty alleviation efforts might succeed if there was equal distribution of land, more literate among poor, fewer low caste households and the local people contested in elections.

Thirtle and Piesse (2007) studied the role of government in agriculture productivity and its effect on poverty reduction in Asia and Sub-Saharan Africa. It was observed that twenty per cent of the world's population or 1.2 billion lived on less than one dollar per day and 70 per cent of them were rural in Asia and Sub-Saharan Africa. The study found that technological change in agriculture generated sufficient productivity growth to give high rates of return in Africa and Asia and in the process, had substantial impact on poverty, whereas productivity growth in industry and services had no impact. The study also showed that government effectiveness was significant in yields and gross domestic product (GDP) and poverty reduction by means of agricultural development.

2.3. Role of Irrigation on Agriculture, Employment and Income

Quite a few well structured studies are available with focus on irrigation and on its different parameters. The article by Bardhan (1973) indicated that irrigation or multiple cropping generated a positive response not only in the wage income but also in the daily wage rate for agricultural labourers. The author also stated that increase in irrigation and cropping intensity raised agricultural wages and agricultural productivity more in an area with a smaller proportion of the rural labour force, dependent on wage employment.

The impact of irrigation on agricultural output and income, within a village, was carried out by Nadkarni (1984). The survey was conducted in 15 villages in South India. Villages were five each from Anantpur district of Andhra Pradesh, Bijapur district of Karnataka and Coimbatore district of Tamil Nadu. Simple regression was used for the analysis. The study area had been mostly under the ryotwari system. The findings of the survey showed that irrigation turned out to be a significant factor behind the cropping intensity in all the three districts, but its impact was rather limited. Irrigation was a weak influence in Bijapur, and not as strong as it was in Anantpur. It was also found that the impact, in terms of improving the income and quality of life, particularly of the poor, was not significant and sometimes even dampening.

Hossain and Sen (1992) analysed the determinants of rural poverty based on secondary information. They pointed out that agriculture was the main source of rural income. It had a direct effect on rural poverty alleviation rather than national economic growth. The agricultural growth was stimulated mainly by rapid diffusion of new technology, particularly modern irrigation. The expansion of irrigation facilitated the growing of an additional crop during the dry season, which considerably reduced rural poverty.

Kerr (1996) attempted to identify the factors that determined differences in performance in agricultural sector and examined the possibilities of influencing those factors. By using the statistical analysis, for agricultural productivity growth, based on all-India district-level data, covering the Indo-Gangetic Plains and Peninsular India, from 1956 to 1990, the author asserted that India's agricultural growth was sufficient to move the country from severe food crises of the 1960s to aggregate food surpluses. Moreover, the increase in agricultural output over the years had taken place under irrigated conditions. Rainfed areas were highly diverse, ranging from resource-rich areas with good agricultural potential to resource-poor areas with much more restricted potential.

Mellor (1996) explained that irrigation was a critical variable influencing the agriculture growth and poverty rates. It was also a significant determinant of overall economic growth rates. Pakistan maintained a growth rate in agricultural GDP of over four per cent for the past two decades due to increased irrigation facilities. Thus, agriculture was able to play a significant and inspiring role in the overall economic growth in Pakistan.

The irrigation paved the way for the adoption of high yielding crop varieties towards the alleviation of poverty in the country. Irrigation not only helped the agricultural production but also played an important role in poverty reduction, both directly and indirectly. Directly, it helped by increasing agricultural production and productivity, especially that of food grains, which in turns helped in eradicating the problems of malnutrition by making food available to the rural poor at affordable prices. Indirectly, irrigation helped in increasing the employment of unemployed landless labourers and small and marginal farmers through its positive impact on cropping intensity and agricultural productivity (Gill and Mustafa, 1997).

Khan (1997) pointed out that agricultural growth was modest and quiet uneven. The agricultural growth has been highly uneven between various regions, even within one Province, particularly between irrigated and without irrigated regions. In addition to that, increased inputs, especially irrigation, were the predominant source to increase not only agricultural production but also crop area, seeds, fertilizers, machinery, credit and agriculture labour. The study also revealed that the increased availability of irrigation water recorded 40 per cent increase in irrigation intensity and 26 per cent in cropping intensity.

Pant (1998) reported that all over the world, irrigation farmers' organisations were very much effective in irrigation management not only at the project level but also at farm levels, which encouraged farmers to act collectively. The study also recorded that the *ahar-pyne* system in South Bihar is one such indigenous irrigation system in India, which has successfully galvanized the local farming community in large numbers against caste divisions and ecological obstacles for over 100 years and ensured equitable distribution of water among individual cultivators and established high growth in agriculture.

Bhattarai *et al.* (2002) quantified the impact of irrigation on agriculture productivity, along with the impact of inputs, other than irrigation, on agriculture productivity. The data were taken during 1970-1993. The study showed, with the help of the regression analysis, that irrigation exercised a positive and significant impact on the agricultural growth and productivity. One per cent increase in irrigated area increased the productivity of all factors about 0.32 per cent in India, from 1970 to 1994. The impact of irrigation was very high when it was compared with the impact of the productivity of other inputs like high yielding varieties of seeds, fertilizer, machinery and other infrastructure.

Palme and Sen (2003) attempted to find out the relationship between irrigation and agriculture growth for 1962-1990 by taking 281 observations. The study showed that the poverty, during 1962-90, was low due to high growth in the agriculture sector and it is evident that irrigation was more important for agricultural growth and poverty alleviation. There was a strong positive correlation between irrigation and agriculture productivity and on the other hand, independent variables such as number of tractors, fertilizers used, number of male labourers, the level of irrigation and the growth in the irrigated area were correlated.

An attempt was made by Narayanamoorthy and Deshpande (2003) to explore the relationship between irrigation development and wage rates of agricultural labourers by using State-wise cross-section data, pertaining to five points of time: 1972-73, 1977-78, 1983, 1987-88 and 1993-94. The results of the study showed that there was positive impact of availability of irrigation on real wages of agricultural labourers. Also irrigation helped to narrow down the differences between the constitutional minimum wages and market wage rates. They also stated that the gender wage differential was found to be narrowing at a faster rate in the States where irrigation was higher.

Skaggs and Samani (2005) studied the relationships between farm size, irrigation practices and on-farm irrigation efficiency in the Elephant Butte Irrigation district, New Mexico. They used 2001 water delivery data, supplied by the irrigated district. The analysis of pecan orchard water delivery data, fieldwork and interviews with irrigators, found that due to the extremely long irrigation durations, inefficient irrigation practices, inadequate on-farm infrastructure, and lack of interest in making improvements to the current irrigation system, there was diminishing law of returns in agricultural growth.

Schultz *et al.* (2005) examined how improvements in water management may contribute to the planned rural developments. The study discussed the population growth and the global distribution of the production of cereals and rice. In order to get an idea about the distribution of the present agricultural production, data over the period

1999-2004, with respect to cereals and rice, were collected (FAO, 1999-2004). The findings of the study revealed that the different means of water management did contribute to increase in food production and enabled sustainable rural development. They suggested that better water management, application of fertilizers and pesticides, soil treatment practices, new varieties and genetic manipulation can contribute to the required increase in yield per hectare and in the process would bring about poverty eradication.

Abdullah (2006) stated in his study that irrigation offers the quickest way of increasing food production, enabling productivity gains through increased yields and increased cropping intensity. Even if 17 per cent of all cultivated land were irrigated, they could produce roughly 40 per cent of the global food output. Consequently, irrigated lands produced twice as much food per unit area as compared to non-irrigated lands. He also suggested increasing food production through productivity gains in order to contribute to hunger eradication, poverty alleviation, national food security and economic development. Moreover, food production faced serious constraints, including declining yield growth rates, natural resource depletion, labour shortages, gender issues, institutional limitations and environmental pollution.

Bhattarai *et al.* (2007) attempted to analyse the difference between direct economic benefits and total economy-wide economic benefits of irrigation development in India. This study employed annual State-level secondary data, across 14 States of India, from 1970 to 1994, to analyse how the irrigation benefits were divided between producers (farmers) and the overall rural economy. These 14 States accounted for more than 90 per cent of the total agrarian economy in India in the early 1990s. By estimating both farm-level benefits and rural economy benefits, authors argued that about two-thirds or more of the benefits from irrigation development reached the non-farm sector in the Indian Economy. They also found that the empirical information on irrigation multipliers derived here, had large implications for public policies such as poverty alleviation and food security in the tropics, where rural livelihoods still largely depend on the productivity and performance of irrigated agriculture.

Irrigation and agricultural sector performance in Odisha and their influence on economic development of the State were studied by Ghosh and Kumar (2010). The analyses of irrigation and agriculture sectors were carried out through literature review, secondary data collection and group discussions with the functionaries. Trends in the growth in irrigation and agriculture sectors were studied over a period. The study revealed that agricultural growth rate of the State was hovering around one per cent. In spite of increase in irrigation potential over the years, foodgrain production in Odisha has showed slower growth. It was yet to reach the production level of 1989-90, with 7.54 and 7.36 million tonnes of food grain production during 2001-02 and 2005-06, respectively. Although, the expected growth rate of irrigated agriculture was not realised, assured irrigation supply had increased rice area during the dry season by 60 per cent. An increase in rice area during the dry season that was 100 per cent irrigated resulted in higher production and productivity in the last couple of years.

2.4. Agricultural Wage Income and Poverty

Many studies are available on agricultural wage income and poverty. Dandekar and Rath (1971) studied the policies and programmes for land reforms to alleviate poverty. As per the result from the study, the major means of production in the Indian Economy is land and irrigation is the vital resource to enhance landuse intensity. Therefore, a suggested remedy to the problem of poverty was to redistribute available land among all those who were dependent upon it and to adopt a labour-intensive technology and investment in irrigation development, with the available amount of capital, to provide employment to agricultural labourers.

Kalpana (1973) used data of 14 major States for period 1956-57 to 1970-71. Simple and multiple regressions were used for the analysis. The study indicated that irrigation or multiple cropping generated a positive response not only in the wage income but also in the daily wage rate for agricultural labourers. It was reported that any increase in irrigation and cropping intensity was likely to raise agricultural wages more in an area with a smaller proportion of the rural labour force dependent on wage employment. The study also showed that the worst possible combination of factors were seen in areas where the labour market was flooded by the virtually landless, the level of agricultural productivity was stagnant and the non-agricultural employment opportunities were too small.

Jose (1973) made an attempt to go in detail into the level, fluctuations and trend of wage rates for agricultural labourers in the whole of Kerala, to see as to what extent the phenomenon was observed in the two districts under the Intensive Agricultural Districts Programme (IADP), during 1962-63 and 1967-68. The basic data used in this connection were largely taken from, *Agricultural Wages in India*, published annually. The two main findings were that the rise in the real wage rate in Kerala between 1960-61 and 1967-68 was far lower than indicated by earlier studies and secondly, there were substantial variations between different villages in the long term movement of real wage rates. The reason for fluctuation of real wages between two villages was the fluctuation in irrigation.

Lal (1976) used data, made available from the 25th round of the National Sample Survey (NSS). The study period was from 1956-57 to 1970-71. The results of the study indicated that real agricultural wages had risen in India during the period 1956-57 to 1970-71. However, in the first part of this period (1956-57 to 1964-65), real wages were constant or dropped in 8 out of the 15 States of India, but in the following period 1964-65 to 1970-71, they had risen sufficiently to offset the earlier decline.

In an attempt to explain the agricultural development and its consequent impact on poverty alleviation, Rao (1978) brought out the fact that there was strong complementary relationship between the growth of agricultural output, employment generation and poverty reduction in Indian agriculture. Further, available evidence showed that when the irrigation potential was fully exploited, the inter-state disparities in development would be low. The author suggested that public and private investment in agricultural inputs, particularly in irrigation, should be stepped up to the maximum, over wide areas in the country to generate larger employment and income for the poorer segments.

Jose (1988) attempted a comparative analysis of agricultural wages in various Indian States from the agricultural year 1970-71 to 1984-85. This was a sequel to an earlier study by the author, which dealt with agricultural wage rates of male workers from 13 States of the Indian Union and covered a period from 1956-57 to 1971-72. The study pointed out those technological changes in agriculture exercised positive influence on agricultural wages. In such a situation, technological changes in agriculture, even without there being any sizeable migration of labour into the agriculturally dynamic regions of the country were likely to have adverse effects on the wage earnings in those regions.

Acharya (1989) used data, drawn from the agricultural wage figures of the Ministry of Agriculture, Government of India, from over 1,000 labour market centres spread over 320 districts in the country to analyse wage rate behaviour. The disaggregated analysis of the study recorded that there was wide and persistent variation in wages across regions, sometimes even within the same States. In general, contiguous regions did not show different wages, but in some cases, the growth of wages in these was quite different. In conclusion, variation in wages had affected the variation in the rural poverty.

Bhalla (1993) dealt with some aspects of wage determination and labour adsorption in Indian agriculture. According to him, there were two major changes taking place in recent years. First, the labour absorptive capacity of Indian agriculture as a whole had declined. Second, the real wages of agricultural labour had at last begun a systematic upward climb. The study suggested that the efforts to push up yields of existing crops by encouraging the increased use of intermediate inputs, especially fertilizers, and by improving agricultural infrastructure, especially irrigation would provide productive jobs in Andhra Pradesh, Gujarat, Karnataka, Maharashtra and Tamil Nadu and the farm labour productivity of Bihar, Odisha and West Bengal would help poverty alleviation.

Banerjee (1993) studied the impact of new economic policies on agricultural labour, using simple regression with secondary data collected from Agricultural Wages in India (AWI). The result of the study indicated that agricultural labour market was quite diversified due to agro-climatic conditions and uneven development of agricultural mode of production. Therefore, the rural poverty persisted highly in agricultural and backward areas. The author suggested that the condition of the rural poor of which agricultural labour was a majority, would improve if their asset holding and entitlement could be increased through land reform and availability of inputs.

Pandey and Kumar (1993), using the analysis of variance technique, studied the variation in real agricultural wage rates between States. Similar type of analysis was done, using data pertaining to different districts of Odisha. The study revealed that there was significant variation in real wage rates over the years. However, the variation over the districts had decreased during the sixties and seventies, but increased marginally during eighties. The relative wage of male labour to female labour had decreased over the period in almost all the districts and recorded negative impact on poverty.

The agriculture continues to be the prime sector of Indian Economy in spite of the rapid progress made in other sectors. Agriculture absorbs the unemployed workforce of the economy. Though a breakthrough in agricultural production technology was made in the mid-1960s, unemployment and under-employment still prevails in agriculture. However, agriculture plays a major role in enhancing employment opportunities, increasing the income of agriculture labourers and reducing rural poverty (Subramanian, 1993).

Similarly, Vaidyanathan (1994) studied the employment situation in rural and urban areas, taking data for 1964-65 and 1974-75 from the Rural Labour Enquiries (RLE). Seventeen major States in India were taken for the study. The study revealed that the unemployment situation in the country had not worsened in the 1970s and 1980s. There was rapid diversification of employment and while the structure of the labour force had changed, leading to a significant rise in the proportion of the workforce depending on wage labour, the conditions of wage labour had not deteriorated as feared. The author also mentioned that agriculture wage employment opportunity exercised major impact on poverty alleviation.

Dev (1995) studied the impact of Employment Guarantee Scheme (EGS) on poverty alleviation aspects in Maharashtra. The study showed that in spite of the limitations in its design and implementation, the EGS had made positive impact on the levels of living of the rural poor in Maharashtra. The author found that the performance of the EGS in terms of employment creation, raising incomes of the poor and checking leakages was much better than any other anti-poverty programmes in India. However, EGS alone cannot remove the entire poverty in rural areas of the State. Still EGS made an attempt to enlarge the scope of employment in order to alleviate poverty in the State.

Tendulkar and Jain (1996) analysed the severity indicators of poverty, between 1983 and 1987-88, for the seventeen major Indian States that account for more than 98 per cent of the total rural population. As per the study, the favourable growth and distributional change effects facilitated improvement in poverty situation, in the drought year of 1987-88, in comparison with an agricultural normal year 1983 at all-India level. It was also found that the dominant and favourable distributional change affected the depth and severity measures of poverty at all-India level due to the broad-based distributional impact of agricultural growth.

Chadha (2001) analysed NSS data on employment, available for five points of time: 27th Round (covering October 1972-September 1973), 32nd Round (July 1977-June 1978), 38th Round (January-December 1983), 43rd Round (July 1987-June 1988), 50th Round (July 1993-June 1994) and 55th Round (July 1999-June 2000). The analysis clearly showed the mixture of gains and losses for rural employment. The employment in agriculture sector was not that significant during pre-reform period as compared to the post-reform period. However, the overall employment of rural workers picked up from an extremely low of 0.33 per cent per annum during 1983 to 1993-94 to 0.66 per cent per annum during the post-reform years. The study concluded that rural employment had suffered greatly in the decade of economic reforms which exercised low effects on rural poverty reduction.

Janvry *et al.* (2005) surveyed 7,333 households of 193 villages, across 39 towns, in six countries, extending from the north to the south in the middle of Hubei Province in China. The analysis of the study showed that rural poverty reduction was generally linked with the role of agriculture in contributing to farm income. However, non-farm employment in rural areas can also be a major contributor. They also found that those who stayed as pure farmers, recorded non-observable characteristics that made them much more productive in agriculture, implying positive selection on these characteristics. Moreover, participation in non-farm activities had a positive spillover effect on household farm production. While farming remained the main source of income for rural households, non-farm income played a more and more significant role in total income.

Khan (2007) analysed the role of employment growth by determining the effect of a given rate of economic growth on the rate of change in poverty. The finding of case studies from 16 countries recently carried out by the United Nations Development Programme (UNDP) and the International Labour Organisation (ILO) was that the rate of poverty reduction had invariably been lower than what it ought to have been. The main reason for this was the low employment intensity of growth.

Rath (2007) examined the links between employment, income and food intake for poor households. The study was conducted in several villages of southern tribal part of Odisha and one village in South Kerala. Data were collected from a total of 120 households with daily details pertaining to time spent by each member, income and food intake. The study showed that in poor households, food intake and the amount of time spent on productive activities went hand in hand. Those who ate more were also seen to be working more. Those who ate less were also seen to be working less. That means that if there were more employment opportunities, there would be more income generations and more food intake by poor households.

By analysing the recent data of the Second Integrated Household Budget Survey 2004-05, Bohne *et al.* (2008) showed that there were considerable differences in agricultural income and rural poverty among the districts in Malawi. They stated that the highest poverty rates and lowest agricultural income were found in the southern districts while the central and northern districts recorded the lowest poverty rates and higher income. The study indicated that the districts with a higher share of households were involved in cash crop and food crops growing, recorded a higher agricultural income and lower poverty headcount.

Many rural households in South-east Asia were able to move out of poverty in the presence of increasing scarcity of farmland, initially by increasing rice income through the adoption of modern rice technology and gradually diversifying their income sources away from farm to non-farm activities (Jonna and Keijiro, 2010). In the concluding remarks, the study found that an important lesson for poverty reduction is to increase agricultural productivity through the development and adoption of modern technology, which subsequently stimulates the development of the non-farm sector, thereby providing employment opportunities for the rural labour force.

Dutta *et al.* (2012) analysed the NSS data for 2011-12 and confirmed that poorer States of India registered more demand for work under the Mahatma Gandhi National Rural Employment Guarantee Scheme (MGNREGS). However, there was considerable unmet demand for work under the scheme in all States and more so in the poorest ones where the scheme was needed most. Nonetheless, the scheme reached the rural poor and backward classes and attracted poor women into the workforce. The study also affirmed that MGNREGS reduced poverty by providing extra employment and income to the poorest in rural areas.

2.5. Agricultural Growth and Rural Poverty Reduction

Good numbers of studies are also available relating agricultural growth to the rural poverty. Ahluwalia (1978) studied the extent and incidence of poverty relating it to the performance of agriculture in India. The author covered an important aspect, taking the time series data from 1956-57 to 1973-74. The first aspect showed a strong correlation between irrigation and agricultural productivity. Second aspect showed that enhanced performance of agriculture reduced poverty in India as a whole. The linear time trend showed that poverty declined in 1956 from 50 per cent to 40 per cent in 1960-61. Poverty increased in 1965 and reached its maximum at 56.6 per cent in 1967. One of the hypotheses of the study was that the agricultural performance reduced poverty. The hypothesis was tested and found that agricultural growth recorded strong inverse relationship with the level of poverty.

Ghosh (1993) examined the working of the factors behind inter-temporal fluctuations in the incidence of rural poverty in West Bengal during 1957-58 to 1986-87. He measured poverty by head-count ratio, with the available data, using regressions. The results of regressions revealed significant inverse relationship between rural poverty and agricultural performance, confirming thereby the existence of trickle down process in rural West Bengal. The result also established the special significance of labour productivity and real wage rate in reducing the incidence of rural poverty over time. Labour productivity, augmenting growth in agriculture, appeared to be more effective in achieving a trend decline in rural poverty than any other that did not increase labour productivity significantly. Therefore, for sustainable reduction in rural poverty, what is required is not merely growth in agriculture, but that type of growth process which enhances labour productivity.

Coxhead and Warr (1995) examined the impact of technical progress in agriculture on changes in measured poverty and aggregate welfare in a developing country. Using a small general equilibrium model, they showed that technical change in agriculture exercised impact on income distribution, poverty reduction and economic welfare within a simple open economy.

Kalman (1995) examined the rural poverty alleviation and agricultural growth in Kerala. The findings of the study indicated that the incidence of rural poverty had declined in the 1980s in spite of the slow rate of growth of the economy in Kerala. In respect of employment, per capita annual employment was declining from 194 and 143 days for male and female agricultural labourers in 1964-65 to 160 and 142 days in 1974-75 and further to 147 and 115 days in

1983-84. According to the study, during the mid-1960s and 1970s, the actual income of agricultural labour households was around half the required income to cross the poverty line whereas with reduced per capita employment, it was nearly 90 per cent in the early 1980s. Even in the absence of State intervention, a sustained process of growth, especially in agriculture, could lead to a decline in poverty through significant changes in the labour market in favour of the poor.

Ghosh (1996), by using cross-section data and covering four points of time (1972-73, 1977-78, 1983 and 1986-87), studied the impact of agriculture development on rural poverty and the impact of other factors on rural poverty in the Indian States. The study showed an inverse relationship between agriculture production and the rural poverty. The other factors, which contributed to rural poverty reduction, were increased employment and the level of real wages.

The result of the study by Rath (1996) showed that since the agriculture is the main stay of the bulk of rural Indians, highly fluctuating agricultural production due to fluctuation in rainfall over the years led to incidence of poverty. Similarly, rapid rises in agricultural production due to growth in irrigated cropped area and use of high-yielding variety seeds, had increased income not only for farmers, but also for the wage earnings labourers and influenced the incidence of rural poverty reduction.

Datt and Ravallion (1997) examined rural poverty rankings of Indian States in 1990, by using pooled State-level data, for the period 1957-91. The study found that trend rates of poverty reduction recorded varying growth rates of farm yield per acre under differing initial conditions. States starting with better infrastructure and human resources witnessed significantly higher long-term rates of poverty reduction.

Datt and Ravallion (1998) took a sample of 24 households, with an average age of 35 years and tried to get an answer to the question. What was the share of the poor people living in the rural areas when agriculture growth took place? They took determinants such as agriculture wages, consumption, poverty measure and food prices for estimation, and came to the conclusion that increase in agriculture productivity not only brought absolute gains but also brought relative benefits to rural poor in India. It also found that a big share in the decline of rural poverty was due to increased wages and low prices of the output.

Ghosh (1998) examined the effects of agricultural development and agrarian structure on rural poverty in West Bengal. The result of the study showed that the changes that had taken place in the agrarian structure, reduced the incidence of rural poverty through the agricultural development channel but at the same time, generated adverse effects on it through the direct distributional channel. Agricultural performance alleviated rural poverty through the trickle down effect. Labour-productivity-augmenting growth in agriculture exercised stronger effect in reducing rural poverty than any other growth process that did not augment labour productivity significantly.

Janvry and Sadoulet (2001) maintained that agricultural technology reduced poverty through direct and indirect effects. Direct effects were gains for the adopters while indirect effects were gains derived from adoption by others leading to lower food prices, employment creation, and growth linkage effects. Results showed that the dominant effect of technology on poverty was through direct effects in Africa, indirect agricultural employment effects in Asia, and linkage effects through the rest of the economy in Latin America.

Luc *et al.* (2006), using poverty data from household surveys of Sub-Saharan Africa, concluded that the direct growth effect of agriculture on poverty reduction was likely to be smaller than that of non-agriculture but the indirect growth effect of agriculture on poverty reduction was substantial. The findings also showed that enhancing agricultural productivity was the critical entry-point in designing effective poverty reduction strategies but to maximise the poverty reducing effects, non-agricultural factors like agricultural technology, investments and institutional organisation of the rural economy must be explained.

Hussain *et al.* (2007) studied population growth, malnutrition, income distribution and poverty in three basins: Limpopo, Nile and Volta. They also discussed the contribution of agriculture to national income and employment generation and poverty reduction. The result of the study explored the strong relationships between agricultural growth, employment growth and poverty alleviation. They suggested that to enhance agricultural productivity and to catalyse agricultural and rural economic growth for effective poverty alleviation, increased public investments in land and water resources development and management are essential.

Sah (2007) studied the chronic poverty in tribal areas of Madhya Pradesh. It has been argued in this study that cause of the chronic poverty in the remote areas was the outcome of complex interactions among social, political and economic forces that affects individuals, households as well as groups. Micro-findings identified the southern tribal belt of Madhya Pradesh to be one of the economically poorest regions in the country due to low agriculture production.

Thorat and Fan (2007) examined the public investment in agriculture and its impact on poverty reduction in rural China and India. The study was carried out during 1993-1997. The study found that growth in agricultural productivity, the rural non-farm sector and rural wages (which were the main sources of poverty reduction in both China and India) were made possible by public investments in rural development, infrastructure (such as roads, power, irrigation, communication and education) and anti-poverty programmes. Nevertheless, returns on these public investments varied drastically across different types of investment in terms of poverty reduction. The trade-off between agricultural growth and poverty reduction was generally limited among different types of investments and between regions. They recommended that agricultural research, education, and infrastructure development would have significant growth impact and also poverty reduction impact.

The agricultural productivity levels and variations in agricultural performance were analysed across districts and regions in the State of Uttar Pradesh, with the aim of identifying factors that affected land and labour productivity and in turn, rural poverty (Pandey and Reddy, 2012). The performance of agriculture in Uttar Pradesh was found to vary considerably across districts and regions, and recorded strong linkages and implications for poverty reduction. Irrigation and fertilizer-use were the major determinants of the level and variations of agricultural productivity in the State. Econometric analysis indicated strong linkages between agricultural productivity and poverty. An increase of 10 per cent in land productivity would reduce poverty by 4.30 per cent. The dependence of workers on agriculture and rural poverty recorded inverse relationship, that is, 10 per cent reduction in labour force could result in 7.70 per cent reduction in poverty.

2.6. Source-wise Impact of Irrigation on Rural Poverty

Although studies relating source-wise irrigation with rural poverty are few in numbers, a few studies have indirectly dealt with this issue.

Shah and Raju (1988) analysed how the working of groundwater markets could influence the small farmers' development. The study examined this by taking data from two similar villages, selected from the West Godavari district of Andhra Pradesh and the Kheda district of Gujarat. The field results showed that groundwater markets had the potential to become powerful instruments for farmers' development and rural poverty reduction. It was also found that groundwater markets not only provided employment opportunities and income to the agricultural labourers of the areas under study, but also helped to reduce the number of poor.

Palmer and Jones (1992) discussed the experiences of Bangladesh with groundwater irrigation, agricultural growth and poverty alleviation. They concluded that development of groundwater in the country led to increased agricultural growth and reduced rural poverty.

The study on Pro-Poor Intervention Strategies in Irrigated Agriculture in Asia (Bangladesh, China, India, Indonesia, Pakistan and Vietnam), was undertaken by the International Water Management Institute (Hussain and Biltonen, 2001). The main objective of this study was to determine realistic options for increasing returns to poor farmers through improving the overall performance of established medium and large-scale surface (canal) irrigation systems. The findings of the study showed that canal irrigation played a major role in poverty reduction, even though the benefits were not always equitable. Canal irrigated agriculture was the main source of food supplies and employment for the poor in Asia. But, the vitality of this sector was declining with growing scarcity and competition for water and increasing over exploitation and degradation of groundwater. The authors suggested that there is an urgent need for policy research and science-based solutions to improve the productivity and sustainability of canal irrigated agriculture, to ensure water-food security for poor men and women which is a critical step in poverty eradication.

Bhattarai and Narayanamoorthy (2003) used the head count ratio measure of poverty to evaluate how the poverty level was affected by input factors like irrigation, adoption of HYVs, fertilizer application, rural literacy rate and rural road density. Data were collected from selected 14 States during the period 1970 to 1993. They found that marginal impact of irrigation, followed by the rural literacy rate, was larger in explaining the variation of rural poverty level in India than those of other factor-inputs selected. Further, the marginal impact of groundwater irrigation on poverty reduction was larger than that of canal irrigation.

Rijsberman (2003) examined the impact of past investments on water resource development and management, irrigation and poverty reduction. By estimating the investments made by private and public sectors in groundwater irrigation, the author noted that private investment on ground water irrigation had larger impact on livelihood of poor people than the public investments in large-scale surface water irrigation systems. Overall, findings of the study showed that past investments in groundwater and surface irrigation development had made a significant contribution to alleviating poverty. However, investments in water resources development, which were considered a high priority by governments and aid agencies for decades, have fallen drastically.

Hussain and Wijerathna (2004) examined the "pro-poor intervention strategies in irrigated agriculture in six Asian countries: Bangladesh, China, India, Indonesia, Pakistan and Vietnam, implemented by the International Water Management Institute (IWMI). The comparative assessments of poverty were undertaken in 26 selected large-scale, medium-scale and canal irrigation systems. The primary household-level data were collected for the agricultural period 2001-02, from selected irrigation systems and adjoining rainfed areas. The study found that poverty situation was worsening where surface-water availability was low, groundwater quality was poor, agricultural productivity was low and opportunities in the non-farm sector were limited. Overall, the findings of the study suggested that by improving land and water productivity of crops, diversifying cropping pattern, improving infrastructure and water distribution across locations, the performance of irrigation systems can be improved which in turn would reduce rural poverty."

Hussain *et al.* (2004) studied the linkages between agricultural water and rural poverty and demonstrated how rural household deprivation of agricultural water triggered other socio-economic deprivations and how improved access could reduce the vulnerability of the poor. The study also analysed the impact of improved community or household access to irrigation on poverty, in large-scale surface irrigation systems in Sri Lanka and Pakistan. A framework for conceptualising the impact of irrigation on rural poverty was provided by taking into account household status as well as the direct and indirect impact of irrigation. The analysis showed that irrigation access allowed poor people to increase their production and income, and enhanced income diversification opportunities, reduced vulnerability caused by seasonality and other factors. There are five key interrelated dimensions of agriculture, water and poverty reduction relationship such as production, income, employment, food security, and overall welfare. The study also found that irrigation's impact on poverty was the highest where landholdings were equitably distributed.

Narayanamoorthy (2007) analysed tank irrigation by using time series data from 1950-51 to 1999-2000. In this study, an attempt was made — (a) to study the growth pattern of tank irrigation across different periods, both at the national as well as across states level; (b) to study the nexus between rainfall and area under tank irrigation at a specific state, and (c) to find out the losers and gainers of tank irrigation among different sizes of farmers. The study found that the area under tank irrigation had declined across different regions in India. The reduction in area under tank irrigation may have negatively impacted agricultural growth and exercised a deleterious effect on resources less marginal and small farmers where a large number of poor people live below poverty line.

In an another study, Narayanamoorthy (2007) examined the nexus between groundwater irrigation and rural poverty by using State-wide cross-sectional data, covering five time points: 1973-74, 1977-78, 1983, 1987-88 and 1993-94. The study showed that there was significant inverse relationship between the availability of groundwater irrigation and the percentage of rural poverty at all five time points. Besides increasing the cropping intensity and productivity of crops, the intensive cultivation of crops, due to the timely access to groundwater irrigation, increased the demand for agricultural labourers and thus the wages rates for those who mostly lived below the poverty line. He stated that both increased affordability of foodgrain and wage rates helped the rural poor to cross the poverty barriers.

Lipton (2007) studied pro-poor intervention strategies in irrigated agriculture in Asia. He showed that 26 major and medium-size canal irrigation schemes in Asia contributed to 20 per cent poverty reduction than adjacent rainfed areas. The gains were more with Pro-Poor Management of Water for Farming (PPMWF) and where the distribution of farmland and farm water was more equal. The important implications of this study for major irrigation in Africa are almost certainly essential for major progress against poverty that needs systematic assessment.

Gandhi and Namboodiri (2009) studied the impact of groundwater irrigation. A total of 25 States in India were selected for the study, spanning from 1950-51 to 2001-02. The study estimated that groundwater was the main source of growth in irrigated area for the past three decades and it now covers over 60 per cent of the irrigated area in the country, producing over 70 per cent of food grain from irrigated agriculture. They also found that the process of managing groundwater resource had very serious implications for the growth and development of the agriculture sector in India as well as the alleviation of poverty in India.

Nayak (2009) highlighted some aspect of inequality in the distribution of land, with regard to accessibility of water extraction devices which led to groundwater depletion and further resulted in disproportionate use of water among different classes of land holders. The author revealed that small and marginal farmers were compelled to utilise less water than their due share and paid higher prices which eventually made them to spend more on groundwater irrigation. This brings out the fact that only by paying higher prices for groundwater, small and marginal farmers were compelled to get food insecurity.

Narayanamoorthy (2010) studied the sustainability of India's groundwater irrigation and observed that the development of groundwater irrigation (GWI) has been very impressive in India, especially after the introduction of the Green Revolution. The study showed that though GWI covered 62 per cent of the net irrigated area today and provided benefits to farmers and played a major role in reducing rural poverty, compared to other sources of irrigation, the continuous exploitation of groundwater had resulted in the drastic drop in the water table and led to sanitization and quality deterioration in different parts of the country. Despite this fact, the groundwater has contributed overwhelmingly to agriculture growth and poverty reduction in rural areas.

2.7. Impact of Irrigation on Rural Poverty Alleviation

Some studies have also studied the impact of irrigation on rural poverty, which are presented in this section. Rao (1987) focused on irrigation impact on small and marginal farmers and agricultural labour households with reference to poverty. The study was carried out in four villages of Gujarat in 1980-81, the year when IRDP was lunched. The findings of the study indicated that rural poverty was reduced due to irrigation, improved tools and extension of new technology undertaken by public body through various rural development programmes. The author suggested the reduction of dependence of the poor on the rural rich through investment on irrigation.

Paul (1990) examined temporal changes in absolute poverty, among farm families in Haryana during the period 1969-70 to 1982-83. The four measures of poverty, namely, family count ratio, head-count ratio, poverty-gap ratio and the Sen Index, were estimated by using the cross-sectional data. The results of the study indicated that (i) there was an increase in the level of poverty among farmers during the seventies but after 1979-80, poverty showed a downward trend; (ii) poverty seems to be associated positively with consumer prices and inversely with the level of per capita income in the region; (iii) incidence of poverty was the highest among small farmers and the second highest among medium farmers; (iv) the large-size farm families recorded the highest incidence of poverty and the small-size farm families displayed the lowest incidence of poverty in all the years; and (v) poverty was inversely related to the level of irrigation in the region.

Hasnip *et al.*, (1999) argued that despite a century of debate and action, and over forty years of international aid to transform the livelihoods of the poor, poverty remains a persistent feature of many developing countries. For many developing countries, increasing agricultural productivity is the key to poverty reduction and irrigation is related to agricultural growth. High economic growth, increased income and improved nutrition were linked to improvements in rural and agricultural development in many countries in Asia between 1970 and 1990. They also showed that irrigated agriculture provided 40 per cent of world food production on only 17 per cent of total cultivated area. They revealed that the irrigated agriculture is the strategy for poverty reduction and there is evidence that this can be achieved. They also suggested from the findings that to increase benefits of irrigated agriculture to the poor, one must understand the real social and economic benefits of irrigation development and the water environment where poor people live.

Agarwal *et al.* (2000), through their intensive household surveys in six villages of Chhattisgarh region under two different ecosystems (irrigated and rainfed), found that income from all economic activities was much higher in irrigated ecosystem than in the rainfed. They demonstrated that the technology-irrigation intensity contributed to higher income, but the larger shares of the income accrued to land and capital. Therefore, adoption of modern technology and the expansion of reliable irrigation exercised significant positive impact on rural poverty in the Chhattisgarh region. It was also found that the incidence, depth, and severity of rural poverty were substantially lower in the irrigated ecosystem than in the rainfed ecosystem.

Narayanamoorthy (2001) made an attempt to understand the role of irrigation on the reduction of the rural poverty and the changing scenario of rural poverty in India, by taking cross-section data of 14 major States from 1972-73 to 1993-94. He demonstrated that irrigation was a crucial factor for agricultural growth as well as rural development. He further stated that the impact of irrigation on poverty can be seen in three ways: (i) supplying of food in lower prices; (ii) increasing wage rates which raised income of the people; and (iii) facilitating more employment opportunities. He further added that there was inverse relationship between irrigation and incidence of rural poverty across States in India.

Bhattarai *et al.* (2002) examined the irrigation impact on income inequality and poverty alleviation. They also examined, specifically poverty issues associated with head-tail water distribution inequity in an irrigation system. They maintained that irrigation had increased crop production and farm income and decreased inequities in income distribution and poverty. The improved access to irrigation infrastructure had increased crop yield, agricultural production and farm income and in turn reduced inequality and rural poverty within a region. In other words, increased crop yield is a necessary condition but not the sufficient condition for poverty alleviation in a region. They pointed out the improved irrigation access to be powerful instrument for reducing rural poverty in a given region.

Bhattarai and Narayanamoorthy (2003) quantified the marginal impact of irrigation and other factor inputs on agricultural productivity and on two key poverty measures across the States. The empirical results showed that there was no significant growth taking place in agriculture productivity when the level of all inputs and their costs were taken together over the last two decades. This productivity growth of all inputs was different from simple crop yield or labour productivity. Analysis of data from 1970 to 1994 for fourteen major States of India, showed that improvement in irrigation and rural literacy rate were the two most important factors for agricultural, growth and rural poverty reduction in India. The study concluded by suggesting that extending access to irrigation to a large number of farmers and investing in human capital development could be crucial to increasing agricultural productivity and reducing poverty in India.

Palmer and Sen (2003) attempted to find out the relationship between irrigation, agriculture growth and poverty by taking 281observations. The study showed that poverty, during 1962-1990, was low due to high growth in the agriculture sector and it is evident that irrigation was more important for agricultural growth and poverty alleviation. The study established a strong correlation between the growth of agriculture sector and the rural poverty in which irrigation paved the way for increased agricultural productivity and the cropped area during the study period. The analysis of the data of poverty and agriculture growth showed that all those Indian States who invested large amount in the agriculture sector had increased agricultural productivity along with reduction in poverty. In other words, there was strong positive correlation between irrigation and agriculture productivity and on the other hand, independent variables such as number of tractors, fertilizers used, number of male labourers, the level of irrigation and the growth in the irrigated area, were correlated.

After reviewing the trends in investments in irrigation, Lipton *et al.* (2003) reached the conclusion that irrigation did have positive impact on the poor. In spite of declining aid to agriculture and falling rates of economic returns to irrigation since the heyday of the 1970s, irrigation remained one of the most crucial inputs into farming. Therefore, it was a potentially important poverty reduction tool during the twenty first century.

Hussain and Hanjra (2003) investigated whether irrigation water mattered for rural poverty alleviation. The findings of the study were: (1) irrigation enabled households to improve crop productivity, grow high-valued crops, generate higher incomes and employment, earn a higher implicit wage rate for family labour and, more importantly, benefit the poor and landless through the enhanced availability of food, lower food prices, higher employment opportunities and income and other indirect effects; (2) access to irrigation water reduced the incidence and severity of poverty; and (3) irrigation's impact on poverty was the highest where landholdings were equitably distributed.

Saleth *et al.* (2003) attempted a quantitative evaluation of the multifarious linkages between irrigation and rural poverty by taking a system approach and using cross-section data pertaining to 80 agro-climatic sub-zones of India for two time points (1984-85 and 1994-95). By estimating and empirically evaluating the mechanics and dynamics of irrigation and poverty linkages, they stated that irrigation's role in reducing rural poverty was substantive. It is now widely recognised that water resources development and management did play a fundamental role in sustainable growth and poverty reduction.

Agricultural intensification through the practice of irrigation as a strategy for poverty reduction was examined by Laurence and Smith (2004). The study pointed four inter-related mechanisms through which irrigated agriculture can reduce poverty. These were improvements in the levels and security of productivity, employment and income for irrigating farm households and farm labour, the linkage and multiplier effects of agricultural intensification for the wider economy, provision of opportunities for diversification of rural livelihoods and multiple uses of irrigation supply. It was concluded that irrigated farming varied widely in its form and impact and possessed diverse local attributes. The study suggested that water resource management decisions must recognise this and be based on holistic and livelihood-centred assessment of irrigation benefits and costs that went beyond food production objectives.

Hussain (2004) studied both qualitative and quantitative approaches to poverty and irrigation relationship by using the field survey data. The study stated that as a vital resource in agriculture, irrigation water contributed to many productive and livelihood activities. The analysis found that irrigation influenced poverty through three pathways: (a) micro-pathway or productivity pathway; (b) meso-pathway or market participation pathway; and (c) macro-pathway or growth pathway. The overall conclusion of these studies was: (i) irrigation had a strong land in augmenting impact on poverty reduction; (ii) indirect impact of irrigation on income and poverty was much larger than direct impacts; and (iii) incidence and severity of poverty were significantly high due to insufficient of irrigation facilities.

Hussain and Hanjra (2004) attempted to analyse the linkages between irrigation and poverty with the help of available studies. The extensive review suggested that there are strong linkages between irrigation and poverty alleviation. These linkages are both direct and indirect. Direct linkages operate through localised and household-level effects and indirect linkages operate through aggregate or national level impacts. Irrigation benefits the poor through higher production, higher yields, lower risk of crop failure, higher and year-round farm and non-farm employment. Irrigation enables small-holders to adopt more diversified cropping patterns and to switch from low-value subsistence production to high-value market-oriented production. Again irrigation investments act as production and supply shifters and have a strong positive effect on growth, benefiting the poor in the long run. Further, irrigation benefits also accrue to the poor and landless in the long run, although in the short run, relative benefits to the landless and land-poor may be small. The study stated that irrigation helped to alleviate both permanent and temporary poverty. In general, irrigation is productivity enhancing, growth promoting and poverty reducing.

Reddy (2004) revealed that despite the development of irrigation in some Northern Telangana districts of Andhra Pradesh such as Nizamabad and Karimnagar, the poor did not benefit from it. Rather, it helped the large farmers to accumulate surpluses only to transfer these and invest in Hyderabad or towns in the districts. On the other hand, the non-poor, who were already on the brink, had fallen into poverty, as lack of irrigation destroyed agriculture and avenues for daily wage income were also not available. The author concluded from the study that development of irrigation alone would not benefit the majority of farmers and landless labourers in Telangana. Hence, there is a need to design specific policies for each district to achieve poverty reduction and also for poverty avoidance.

Hussain and Hanjra (2004) addressed two important questions: (a) What is the role of irrigation development and management in poverty alleviation? and (2) What are the linkages and pathways through which irrigation could contribute to poverty? The authors, by analysing the secondary data with descriptive analysis, found the answers to the above two questions. Further, the authors demonstrated that there were strong linkages between irrigation and rural poverty.

Molden *et al.* (2007) stated that effective irrigation service provided the environment for productive and sustainable agriculture income, employment, economic growth and lifting people from poverty and keeping them out of poverty. On the other hand, poorly managed irrigation experienced opposite effects. The study suggested that for poverty alleviation, there is need to give due attention to the people dependent on irrigation water including the landless, livestock keepers, fishermen and domestic water users.

Hussain (2007), using primary data collected from 5400 rural households of 26 irrigation systems, analysed the links between irrigation and poverty alleviation in six Asian countries (India, Pakistan, Bangladesh, China, Vietnam and Indonesia). The author expressed that irrigation was an essential part of the package of technologies, institutions and policies that increased agricultural output in Asia. However, the analysis showed that this package did not yet fully succeed in banishing poverty.

Magistro *et al.* (2007) related the field experience of an international Non-Governmental Organisation (NGO) in strengthening linkages between irrigation development and poverty reduction. Poverty Reduction through Irrigation and Small-holder Markets (PRISM) was introduced as a methodology for combining small-plot irrigation technology with complementary inputs and services to enhance small farmers' ability to participate effectively in markets for high-value agricultural commodities. Data from field projects in Nepal and India indicated that PRISM led to significant additional income for small farmers and other micro and small enterprises in agricultural value chains. It also explored some important implications for major irrigation system and systematic assessment in Africa for important progress against poverty.

The main objective of the study by Gurunathan (2008) was to understand groundwater irrigation and rural poverty nexus in the State of Tamil Nadu. To analyse the independent strength of irrigation in determining the rural poverty, simple linear regression was computed by using Ordinary Least Squares (OLS) method, involving irrigated area IAPTRP (Irrigation Area Per Thousand Rural Population) as an explanatory variable and the percentage rural poverty as dependent variable. The result shows that there was significant inverse relationship between irrigation and rural poverty. An increase of one hectare in irrigated area reduced about 0.49 per cent of rural poverty from the mean. The variable GIAGCA (Percentage of Gross Irrigated Area to Gross Cropped Area) turned out to be positive and significant. The coefficient of IAPTRP implies that the rural poverty can be reduced by 1.54 per cent through an increase of one hectare of groundwater irrigation for every thousand rural population. Further, to understand the role of irrigation in determining poverty, multiple regressions (OLS method) was computed by including other variables which were considered to be important in explaining the variation in rural poverty. Findings of the study indicated that out of five variables included in the multiple regressions, irrigation was found predominantly and significantly strong in determining rural poverty.

Simon *et al.* (2009) examined the linkages between water and food systems in six river basins. The purpose of analysing poverty with respect to water use is threefold: first, to define the links between water, agricultural water use and poverty; second, to understand and quantify the precise nature of problems, as they occur within basins; and, third, to identify opportunities for interventions, based on analysis of the opportunities and risks. The findings of the study indicated that agriculture remained the predominant water user, but the linkage between water, agriculture and livelihoods was more complex.

Schultz *et al.* (2009) studied the role of water management in securing global food security and poverty alleviation. The findings of the study revealed that most of the poverty exists in rural areas of emerging and least developed countries. The study concluded that the access to irrigation improved agricultural production at lower level costs and further enabled poverty alleviation. They also suggested that to maintain food security in the near and medium term future (coming 25-30 years), a substantially larger increase in production by enhancing irrigation system will be required than continuation of the present trend.

Having taken a sample of 613 farm households, from both irrigators and non-irrigators, Gebrehaweria *et al.* (2009) studied the development of irrigation schemes as a strategy of poverty reduction in Tigray. They found that the average income of non-irrigating households was less than that of the irrigating households by about 50 per cent. The overall average income gain due to access to irrigation ranged from 4000 Birr to 4500 Birr per household per annum. Also they found that farming income was more important to irrigating households than to non-irrigating households, and off-farm income was negatively related with access to irrigation. The authors finally concluded that irrigation enhanced income of the household and reduced rural poverty.

Since Agricultural Water Productivity (AWP) is considered by many as a valuable concept that links agricultural water use to the benefits in terms of food or income, Cook *et al.* (2009) reviewed various case studies from four river basins and elsewhere. The analysis found that AWP and poverty were related but that the strength of the relationship and its nature varied with scale. At the global scale, improved water productivity will enable an expanding global population to feed itself from a finite water resource. At the local scale, improved water productivity is more often a consequence of other changes such as crop productivity or value. It is also found that there was no evidence of causal linkages between agricultural water consumption and poverty due to the absence of clear definitions of the links between water use by multiple factors and the outcomes produced.

Narayanamoorthy and Hanjra (2010) used cross-section data relating to seven time points from 1973-74 to 2004-05 pertaining to 29 districts of Tamil Nadu to study the determinants of poverty. The study found that there was a wide variation in urban rural poverty between the districts having above and below the State average. The incidence of rural poverty was significantly less among Districts having Irrigation Above the State Average (DIASA) group of districts as compared to Districts having Irrigation Below the State Average (DIBSA) group of districts suggesting that irrigation helped in reducing rural poverty in Tamil Nadu. The study also showed that though the disparity in rural-urban poverty had narrowed in Tamil Nadu as compared to other States of India, there was still wide disparity between rural-urban poverty across the districts of Tamil Nadu. They further stated that it is possible to reduce simultaneously, both rural and urban poverty, with assured irrigation facility.

Ghosh *et al.* (2011) analysed irrigation, agriculture and level of living in the districts of Odisha. District-wise scenario of irrigation, agriculture and living standard were studied with the help of different indices developed for the study like groundwater development, irrigation coverage index, composite irrigation index, agricultural development index, level of living index and poverty ration index. The study delineated the links or missing links between irrigation resources, agriculture development, poverty and level of living in the districts of Odisha which was explained through a correlation matrix. Agricultural development index was significantly related with composite irrigation index, while level of living was significantly related with irrigation, agriculture and poverty indices. The regression analyses revealed that 71 per cent variation in agricultural development index could be explained by composite irrigation index. In other words, irrigation development had impacted rural poverty.

Ghosh *et al.* (2012) carried out an analysis of irrigation, agriculture, livelihood and poverty linkages in the districts of Odisha. The study found that half the districts recorded medium values of agricultural development Index. Level of living in majority of districts was found at the medium level. About 60 per cent of the Below Poverty Line (BPL) rural families comprised agricultural labourers, marginal and small farmers ranging from 25 to 94 per cent. Some districts displayed higher irrigation and higher agricultural development and some recorded lower irrigation and lower agricultural development. Lower groundwater exploitation for irrigation in Odisha was attributed to the lower impact of irrigation development on the poverty and livelihood scenario. The links among irrigation, agriculture and poverty were found more in the case of poorer condition of different sectors while betterment in one sector was not linked to betterment of other sector in many of the districts.

2.8. Concluding Remarks

The existing studies show that irrigation and rural poverty are closely related both directly as well as indirectly. Majority studies maintained that irrigation increased the agricultural productivity, while a few other studies recorded that increased agricultural productivity led to poverty alleviation in many developed countries including India. There are also studies available regarding the role of irrigation on agriculture income, employment opportunity and rural poverty alleviation. A few relevant studies have analysed the importance of irrigation on rural poverty reduction. There are limited studies available on the nexus between irrigation development and rural poverty, except Narayanamoorthy (2001) who used secondary data at macro-level. There are absolutely no studies available about the irrigation development and its impact on rural poverty reduction, for the study period 1973-74 to 2011-12 covering various States in India. Studies are also not available covering district-level data on the issue of irrigation and rural poverty nexus. Detailed studies are also not available about the impact of irrigation by sources on rural poverty. Therefore, keeping this in view, an attempt has been made in this study to analyse the relationship between irrigation and rural poverty by using both macro and micro-level data.

3
Data and Methodology

3.1. Introduction

This chapter presents the methodology which was used for conducting this study. Research methodology is an art of scientific investigation as it finds out the various tools and techniques for the research work. It lends helping hand for the researcher to use both primary as well as secondary data, according to the needs of the research work. The present study on irrigation and rural poverty was carried out using both macro and micro-level data. The macro-level analysis was conducted by using secondary data, collected from various sources and micro-level analysis was conducted using primary data, collected from the field survey. The details of data coverage and the models used for studying the nexus between irrigation and rural poverty are provided in this chapter.

3.2. Universe of the Study Area

India is one of the developing countries in the world located in South Asia. It is the seventh largest country by area, the second most populous country, with over 1.21 billion people and the most populous democracy in the world. India is delimited by the Indian Ocean on the South, the Arabian Sea on the South-West, and Bay of Bengal on the South-East. It shares land borders with Pakistan to the West; China, Nepal, and Bhutan to the North-East; and Burma and Bangladesh to the East.

The Indian Economy is the world's eleventh largest by GDP and third largest by Purchasing Power Parity (PPP). Following market based economic reforms in 1991; India became one of the fastest-growing major economies, which is considered a newly industrialised country. It has the third largest standing army in the world and ranks eighth in military expenditure among nations. However, it continues to face the challenges of poverty, malnutrition, inadequate public health care etc.

India is a federal constitutional republic and democratic country, consisting 640 districts in 29 States and 7 Union Territories (Census of India, 2011). Out of 29 States, 14 major States, namely, Andhra Pradesh, Bihar, Haryana, Gujarat, Karnataka, Kerala, Madhya Pradesh, Maharashtra, Odisha, Punjab, Rajasthan, Tamil Nadu, Uttar Pradesh, and West Bengal, were taken for the State-level study in India. Out of 640 districts, 178 districts from 13 major States were taken for the district-level study on the issue of irrigation and poverty nexus. For the micro-level study, four villages from the Aranthangi taluk were selected. Aranthangi is one of the taluks in Pudukkottai district of Tamil Nadu in India.

3.3. Sample Size and Sampling Procedure

There are 756 villages in the study area (Pudukkottai district) and it was difficult to include all those villages in the study. Out of 756 villages in the district, four villages were selected as the study area. These four villages are under Aranthangi taluk of Pudukkottai district in the State of Tamil Nadu, India. The selected four villages were Ayangudi, Kallakudi, Kullathur and Veeramangalam. The following procedures were followed to select these villages. Firstly, the distance from Aranthangi town to each village was more or less the same. The reason for focusing on distance was that the socio-economic condition of Aranthangi town influenced these villages equally. Secondly, these villages were selected on the basis of irrigation sources to understand which of the irrigation source was impacting rural poverty reduction significantly. Therefore, Ayangudi was selected as the Groundwater Irrigated Village (GIV), Kalakudi as the Canal Irrigated Village (CIV), and Kulattur as the Tank Irrigated Village (TIV) and Veeramangalam as the Rainfed/Un-irrigated Village (RFV). The logic behind this selection of RFV was to compare the percentage of households below poverty line and percentage of population below poverty line with irrigated villages. Thirdly, all the four villages were selected on the grounds that the cropping pattern of these villages was almost similar because they cultivated more or less the same crops. Fourthly, in each sample village, agricultural labour households were identified predominantly than other types of households. The core season for focusing on agricultural labour households was that, as mentioned earlier, the rate of poverty was high among the agricultural labour households. Out of the agricultural labour households, 50 sample respondents were selected for the study. Fifthly, these villages are located in the vicinity of Aranthangi town which is just 35 km. from the University. Similarly, various other points were kept in consideration while selecting these villages.

These villages were selected after visiting them many times. After a lot of discussion with the respective village people and investigating for more than two months about the villages, these villages were selected. A list of agricultural labour households was collected from the Village Assistant Officers (VAO) of respective sample villages and then systematic random sampling method was used to select sample respondents. By taking 50 labour households from each sample village, a total of 200 labour households from these villages were taken as samples for this study. For the purpose of collecting information from the sample respondents, the heads of sample households were interviewed. In case a respondent had no time or refused to be interviewed, head of the next household was interviewed. This was helpful in reducing the sample bias and in collecting reliable information.

Before going to collect the information from the sample respondents of agricultural labour households, a well structured interview schedule was formulated to collect the required information for the study. Before initiating the sample survey, a pilot survey was designed to gather reliable data required for this study. The pilot survey was done from a sample of five respondents from each selected villages. After pilot survey, the interview schedule was modified in the light of feedback received from the sample respondents of agricultural wage labourers. Some of the irrelevant questions were deleted and other necessary questions were included in the revised version of the interview schedule. The data were collected from the respondents pertaining to the year 2013-14.

3.4. Data Sources

As mentioned earlier, both primary and secondary data were used in this study. Primary data were used to study the relationship between poverty and source-wise irrigation, which is called the micro-level study. Secondary data were used to study the impact of irrigation on rural poverty, at both State-level and district-level, across India, which is called macro-level study.

In the State-level study, it was proposed to capture the variations in the incidence of rural poverty across the States and therefore, 14 major States of India were covered for the analysis. The 14 major States selected for the analysis were Andhra Pradesh, Bihar, Gujarat, Haryana, Karnataka, Kerala, Madhya Pradesh, Maharashtra, Odisha, Punjab, Rajasthan, Tamil Nadu, Uttar Pradesh and West Bengal. These major States altogether accounted for about 95 per cent of the total population, below the poverty line in rural India, both in the early seventies (1973-74) and also in the second decade of post-liberalisation (2011-12). The percentage of rural population below the poverty line, released by the Planning Commission for eight different time points, namely 1973-74, 1977-78, 1983, 1987-88, 1993-94, 1999-2000, 2004-05 and 2011-12, were used as the main data source for this study (Planning Commission, 2014). The other variables, considered for the analysis, were State-wide data relating to percentage of gross irrigated area to gross cropped area (GIAGCA), irrigated area (ha) per thousand rural population (IAPTRP), real wage rate (Rs.) of agricultural labourers (RWAL), productivity (kg) of food grains (PFG), State domestic product (Rs.) of agriculture per head of rural population (SDAPHRP), cropping intensity (CI) and food grains production (kg.) per head of rural population (FPHRP). These data were compiled from published sources such as Indian Agricultural Statistics, Area and Production of Principal Crops in India (both are published by the Ministry of Agriculture, Government of India, New Delhi), Census of India, Fertilizer Statistics (published by the Fertilizer Association of India) and also from some of the recent published materials.

Similarly, in the district-level study, the analysis was based on secondary data. The study covered 178 districts drawn from 13 States in India, namely Andhra Pradesh (15 districts), Bihar (6 districts), Gujarat (10 districts), Haryana (6 districts), Karnataka (13 districts), Madhya Pradesh (28 districts), Maharashtra (16 districts), Odisha (9 districts), Punjab (11 districts), Rajasthan (19 districts), Tamil Nadu (6 districts), Uttar Pradesh (28 districts) and West Bengal (11 districts). These 178 Districts were selected without any specific reasons. As the comparable data for the 178 districts for all the four time points (1970-71, 1980-81, 1990-91 and 2000-01) were available for the analysis the remaining districts were not included for the analysis.

The data for district-level study were compiled from various sources. Since this study was based on the assumed nexus between rural poverty and irrigation, the main data on Percentage of Rural Poverty (PRP), for the year 2004-05, were collected from Choudhuri and Gupta (2009) and the data on Percentage of Gross Irrigated Area to Gross Cropped Area (GIAGCA) were compiled from various issues of Indian Agricultural Statistics, published by the Ministry of Agriculture, Government of India, New Delhi. Gross Cropped Area Per Thousand Rural Populations (GCAPTRP) was compiled and estimated from Bhalla and Singh (2010, 2011) and Census of India (GoI, 1971, 1981, 1991 and 2001). District-wise data on Cropping Intensity (CI) were collected from Bhalla and Singh (2011). Data on rural literacy (LITE), availability of *pucca* road (ROAD), villages electrified (ELEC) were computed from various issues of Census of India for the years 1971, 1981, 1991 and 2001. Average wages of skilled and unskilled rural male labourers were taken from Agriculture wages in India (AWI) for various years.

For the micro-level analysis, as mentioned earlier, field survey data for the year 2013-14 were used. The main objective of this study was to analyse the source-wise impact of irrigation on rural poverty. To achieve this objective, four sample villages were selected based on irrigation source, namely Ayangudi, Kalakudi, Kulattur and Veeramangalam. Ayangudi was considered as a Groundwater Irrigated Village (GIV), Kalakudi was a Canal Irrigated Village (CIV), Kulattur was a Tank Irrigated Village (TIV), and Veeramangalam was treated as a Rainfed Village (RFV). These four villages are in Aranthangi taluk, which comes under Pudukkottai district of Tamil Nadu in India.

For the purpose of analysis, the random sampling techniques were followed to select 50 samples of respondents from each village. The sample respondents were selected specifically from the agricultural wage labour households because most of the poor people were found in the agricultural labour households which were suitable for the study.

Percentage of Households Below Poverty Line (PHBPL) and Percentage of Population Below Poverty Line (PPBPL) were considered as poverty variables. Poverty was estimated by using consumption expenditure, as suggested by Tendukar Committee (Planning Commission, 2013). Firstly, Monthly Per Capita Consumption Expenditure (MPCE) was estimated by dividing the total consumption expenditure of sample households by the total population of those particular households. Secondly, Monthly Per Capita Consumption Expenditures (MPCEs) were arranged in an ascending order. Thirdly, according to the rural poverty line (Rs. 880) of Tamil Nadu (Planning Commission, 2013), the PMCEs which were higher than Rs. 880 were deemed to be above the poverty line and those MPCEs below Rs. 880, were regarded as below the poverty line. This method of calculating rural poverty was used equally for all the four sample villages which were selected for the study.

Wage Rate of Agricultural Labourer (WRAL) used in the analysis was defined as the average wage rate per day received by male and female. It explains the level of income of the households. Average Employment Days (AED) was used to reflect employment opportunities for the people. Dependency Ratio (DR) reflects how many people were depending on the working people in those households. If the number of dependent people were more than the number of working population, then poverty must be prevalent in those households.

Monthly Per Capita Consumption Expenditure (MPCE) is an important variable with which the poverty in India has been measured or estimated. If the MPCE is lower than the State rural poverty line fixed by the Planning Commission (2013), it is regarded that they are under below poverty line. Monthly Per Capita Income (MPI) is another important variable for poverty defining because normally MPCE dependent on income. Percentage of Farm Wage to Total Wage Income (PFWTWI) and Percentage of Non-Farm Wage to Total Wage Income (PNFWTWI) were also included as variables for analysis to understand which of the two variables was more pronounced in determining poverty.

3.5. Procedures for Data Analysis

Similar to the data sources, the procedures for data analysis also consisted of two types, viz., macro-level and micro-level analysis. The macro-level study covered both State and district-level data across India. At the State-level analysis, one of the objectives of the study was to analyse the relationship between irrigation development and rural poverty across the major States in India. Therefore, in the first step of the analysis, States were divided into two groups, based on the level of poverty, as States with Above National Average in rural poverty (ANA) and States with Below National Average in rural poverty (BNA). This was done to understand the trends in rural poverty and irrigation across different States.

Second, in order to know the strength of correlation between rural poverty and other poverty determinant variables (RWAL, PFG, SDAPHRP, CI and FPHRP) including irrigation variables (IAPTRP and GIAGCA), correlation values were computed.

Third, apart from studying the nexus between irrigation development and rural poverty determinant variables, an attempt was also made to study the trends in the degree of relationship between irrigation and rural poverty, the impact of base-level irrigation on rural poverty and also to identify whether the relationship between the two was weakening or strengthening due to changes in the other poverty determining factors. In order to find out this relationship between irrigation and rural poverty, three different types of simple linear regressions (OLS method) were computed by treating PRP (Percentage of Rural Poverty) as the dependent variable and IAPTRP (Irrigation Area Per Thousand Rural Populations) as an explanatory variable. The explanatory variable (IAPTRP) was used without any time lag, with 5 year time lag and also with 10 year time lag for all the time points. The simple regression equations estimated for the analysis are:

$$PRP_t = \alpha + b_1 \, IAPTRP_t \qquad \ldots (1)$$
$$PRP_t = \alpha + b_1 \, IAPTRP_{t-5} \qquad \ldots (2)$$
$$PRP_t = \alpha + b_1 \, IAPTRP_{t-10} \qquad \ldots (3)$$

Where,

PRP_t = per cent of rural poverty in time t,
IAPTRP = irrigated area per thousand rural population in time t, in time t–5 and in time t–10,
b_1 = regression parameter to be estimated,
α = constant.

Similar to the State-level analysis, the study proposed to demonstrate the impact of irrigation on PRP (Percentage of Rural Poverty) across districts in India. The first method used in this study to analyse the relationship between irrigation and rural poverty, was the descriptive analysis. The descriptive analysis describes the characteristics of districts and variables selected for the analysis.

The second method to study the nexus between irrigation development and rural poverty was the simple regression analysis. Four different types of simple linear regressions (OLS method) were computed (equations 4, 5, 6 and 7), keeping PRP (Percentage of Rural Poverty) as the dependent variable and GIAGCA (Percentage of Gross Irrigated Area to Gross Cropped Area) as an explanatory variable. Out of four simple regressions, equation (4) was used to study the impact of irrigation on rural poverty, treating PRP as the dependent variable and GIAGCA as the independent variable at four time points. Three more regressions (equations: 5, 6 and 7) were used to study the impact of base level irrigation on rural poverty, keeping PRP as the dependable variable and GIAGCA as the independent variable, with 10, 20 and 30 year time lag for all time points. Lagged variables were used in regression analysis to know how best the base-level irrigation influenced rural poverty. The following equations were used for the regression analysis:

$$PRP_t = \alpha + b_1 GIAGCA_t \qquad \ldots (4)$$
$$PRP_t = \alpha + b_1 \, GIAGCA_{t-10} \qquad \ldots (5)$$
$$PRP_t = \alpha + b_1 \, GIAGCA_{t-20} \qquad \ldots (6)$$
$$PRP_t = \alpha + b_1 \, GIAGCA_{t-30} \qquad \ldots (7)$$

Where,

PRP_t = percentage of rural poverty in time t,
$GIAGCA_t$ = percentage of irrigated area to cropped area in time t, in time t–10, t–20 and in time t–30 in time t, in time t–10, t–20 and in time t–30,
b_1 = regression parameter to be estimated,
α = constant.

After studying independent relationship between irrigation and rural poverty, multiple regression analysis was carried out. The multiple regression analysis was used to identify as to which of the variable greatly and significantly influenced the rural poverty. Similar to the simple regression, four different types of multiple regressions were computed. The first multiple regression, in equation (8), was estimated keeping PRP variable as the dependent variable and other selected poverty determinants variables (CI, ELE, GCAPTRP, GIAGCA, LITE ROAD and WAGE) as independent variables (without time lag) to identify which of the poverty determinants variable was predominantly influenced rural poverty. Other three multiple regressions presented in equations (9), (10) and (11), were carried out by treating PRP as the dependent variable and other poverty determinants variables (CI, ELE, GCAPTRP, GIAGCA, LITE ROAD and WAGE) as explanatory variables, with time lag 10, 20 and 30 years, for all the four times. Lagged variables were used in regression analysis to identify how best the base level poverty determinant variables influenced rural poverty. The regression models, used to study the influence of poverty determinant variables on the rural poverty, are as follows:

$$PRP_t = \alpha + b_1CI_t + b_2ELE_t + b_3GCAPTRP_t + b_4GIAGCA_t + b_5LITE_t + b_6ROAD_t + b_7WAGE_t \quad \ldots (8)$$

$$PRP_t = \alpha + b_1CI_{t-10} + b_2ELE_{t-10} + b_3GCAPTRP_{t-10} + b_4GIAGCA_{t-10} + b_5LITE_{t-10} + b_6ROAD_{t-10} + b_7WAGE_{t-10} \quad \ldots (9)$$

$$PRP_t = \alpha + b_1CI_{t-20} + b_2ELE_{t-20} + b_3GCAPTRP_{t-20} + b_4GIAGCA_{t-20} + b_5LITE_{t-20} + b_6ROAD_{t-20} + b_7WAGE_{t-20} \quad \ldots (10)$$

$$PRP_t = \alpha + b_1CI_{t-30} + b_2ELE_{t-30} + b_3GCAPTRP_{t-30} + b_4GIAGCA_{t-30} + b_5LITE_{t-30} + b_6ROAD_{t-30} + b_7WAGE_{t-30} \quad \ldots (11)$$

Where,

PRP_t = percentage of rural poverty in time t,

CI_t = cropping intensity in time t, in time t–10, t–20 and in time t–30,

$GCAPTRP_t$ = gross cropped area to per thousand rural population in time t, in time t–10, t–20 and in time t–30,

$GIAGCA_t$ = percentage of irrigated area to cropped area in time t, in time t–10, t–20 and in time t–30,

$LITE_t$ = percentage of villages electrified in time t, in time t–10, t–20 and in time t–30,

$ROAD_t$ = percentage of villages having road facilities in time t, in time t–10, t–20 and in time t–30

$WAGE_t$ = average wages of skilled and unskilled rural male labourers in time t, in time t–10, t–20 and in time t-30, b_1= regression parameter to be estimated, α = constant.

For the micro-level analysis, primary data were used to study the impact of source-wise irrigation on rural poverty. As reported earlier, primary data were collected from four villages in Aranthangi taluk, which is under Pudukkottai district of Tamil Nadu in India. for the purpose of the analysis, four villages were selected based on the sources of irrigation. India has mainly three types of irrigation sources such as well irrigation, canal irrigation and tank irrigation. The three villages were selected, based on the irrigation sources and another one village was selected as rainfed area. Thus, a total of four villages were selected for the study. Out of four villages selected, Ayangudi was classified as Groundwater Irrigated Village (GIV), Kalakudi as Canal Irrigated Village (CIV), Kulattur as Tank Irrigated Village (TIV) and Veeramangalam was Rainfed or dry land Village (RFV). As followed in macro-level analysis, both descriptive and regression analysis were employed for studying the nexus between irrigation and rural poverty at micro-level.

At the outset, the characteristics of sample villages, sample households and sample respondents were investigated by using the descriptive analysis. Second, two types of regression analysis (simple and multiple regressions) were performed to explain the relation between source-wise irrigation and rural poverty. To establish the independent relationship between source-wise irrigation and rural poverty, different types of simple regressions were used, without considering any other poverty determining variable except source-wise irrigation variable. Simple regressions were used to study the variation of PPBPL within source-wise irrigated villages, between source-wise irrigated village and un-irrigated village. The variable PPBPL is used as the dependent variable and source-wise irrigation variable as independent variable to study the source-wise impact of irrigation on rural poverty. In order to represent the source-wise irrigation variable in the analysis, D_i (DUMMY) variable was included as the irrigation variable. The regression equations are as follows:

$$PPBPL = \alpha + b_1 D_i + e_i \quad \ldots (12)$$

Where,

PPBPL = percentage of population below poverty line,

D_i = irrigation dummy (GIV=1 and CIV=0),
b_1 = regression parameter to be estimated,
α = constant,
e_i = error term.

In equation (12), to examine the variation of poverty in Groundwater Irrigated Village (GIV) and Canal Irrigated Village (CIV), PPBPL was considered as dependent variable and D_i (irrigation dummy) was the independent variable. The irrigation variable was considered as DUMMY variable (D_i) for the analysis where GIV=1 and CIV=0.

$$PPBPL = \alpha + b_1 D_i + e_i \qquad \ldots (13)$$

Where,

PPBPL = percentage of population below poverty line,
D_i = irrigation dummy (GIV=1 and TIV=0),
b_1 = regression parameter to be estimated,
α = constant,
e_i = error term.

In equation (13), to examine the variation of poverty in Groundwater Irrigated Village (GIV) and Tank Irrigated Village (TIV), PPBPL was considered as dependent variable and D_i (irrigation dummy) was the independent variable. The irrigation variable was considered as DUMMY variable (D_i) for the analysis where GIV=1 and TIV=0.

$$PPBPL = \alpha + b_1 D_i + e_i \qquad \ldots (14)$$

Where,

PPBPL = percentage of population below poverty line,
D_i = irrigation dummy (CIV = 1 and TIV = 0),
b_1 = regression parameter to be estimated,
α = constant,
e_i = error term.

In equation (14), to examine the variation of poverty in Canal

Irrigated Village (CIV) and Tank Irrigated Village (TIV), PPBPL was considered as dependent variable and D_i (irrigation dummy) was the independent variable. The irrigation variable was considered as DUMMY variable (D_i) for the analysis where CIV=1 and TIV=0.

$$PPBPL = \alpha + b_1 D_i + e_i \qquad \dots (15)$$

Where,

PPBPL = percentage of population below poverty line,
D_i = irrigation dummy (GIV = 1 and RFV = 0),
b_1 = regression parameter to be estimated,
α = constant,
e_i = error term.

In equation (15), to examine the variation of poverty in Groundwater Irrigated Village (GIV) and Rainfed Village (RFV), PPBPL was considered as dependent variable and D_i (irrigation dummy) was the independent variable. The irrigation variable was considered as DUMMY variable (D_i) for the analysis where GIV=1 and RFV=0.

$$PPBPL = \alpha + b_1 D_i + e_i \qquad \dots (16)$$

Where,

PPBPL = percentage of population below poverty line,
D_i = irrigation dummy (CIV = 1 and RFV = 0),
b_1 = regression parameter to be estimated,
α = constant,
e_i = error term.

In equation (16), to examine the variation of poverty in Canal Irrigated Village (CIV) and Rainfed Village (RFV), PPBPL was considered as dependent variable and D_i (irrigation dummy) was the independent variable. The irrigation variable was considered as DUMMY variable (D_i) for the analysis where CIV = 1 and RFV = 0.

$$PPBPL = \alpha + b_1 D_i + e_i \qquad \dots (17)$$

Where,

PPBPL = percentage of population below poverty line,
D_i = irrigation dummy (TIV = 1 and RFV = 0),
b_1 = regression parameter to be estimated,
α = constant,
e_i = error term.

In equation (17), to examine the variation of poverty in Tank Irrigated Village (TIV) and Rainfed Village (RFV), PPBPL was considered as dependent variable and D_i (irrigation dummy) was the independent variable. The irrigation variable was considered as DUMMY variable (D_i) for the analysis where TIV=1 and RFV=0.

After estimating different types of simple regressions analysis to explain the relation between source-wise irrigation and rural poverty, regression was computed to establish the independent relationship between irrigation and rural poverty by treating PPBPL as the dependent variable and irrigations (GIV, CIV and TIV) variable as independent variable. In order to represent the irrigation variable in the analysis, D_i (DUMMY) variable was included as the irrigation variable. The regression equation used for estimating is as follows:

$$PPBPL = \alpha + b_1 D_i + e_i \qquad \dots (18)$$

Where,

PPBPL = percentage of population below poverty line,
D_i = irrigation dummy (GIV = 3, CIV = 2, TIV = 1 and RFV = 0),
b_1 = regression parameter to be estimated,
α = constant,
e_i = error term.

In equation (18), to examine variation of poverty in irrigated villages (GIV, CIV and TIV) and Rainfed Village (RFV), PPBPL was considered as dependent variable and D_i (irrigation dummy) was the independent variable. The irrigation variable was considered as DUMMY variable (D_i) for the analysis where GIV=3, CIV=2, TIV=1 and RFV=0.

After analysing the independent relationships between the

different sources of irrigation and rural poverty, multiple regression analysis was performed to understand which of the selected poverty determinant variables played a major role in influencing rural poverty and what was the strength of association between irrigation and rural poverty. Therefore, multiple regression was estimated considering, PPBPL as the dependent variable and other poverty determinant variables, including irrigation variable, as independent variables. The regression equation used for the analysis is as follows:

$$PPBPL = \alpha + b_1 AED + b_2 DR + b_3 FS + b_4 MPI + b_5 PNFWTWI + b_6 WRAL + b_7 D_i + e_i \quad \ldots(19)$$

Where,

PPBPL = percentage of population below poverty line,
AED = average employment days/month/person,
DR = dependency ratio (%),
FS = family size (number of person),
MPI = monthly per capita income (Rs.),
PNFWTWI = percentage of non-farm wage to total wage income,
WRAL = wage rate of agricultural labourers/day,
D_i = irrigation dummy (GIV=3, CIV=2, TIV=1 and RFV=0),
b_1 = regression parameter to be estimated,
α = constant,
e_i = error term.

In equation (19), PPBPL was the dependent variable and other variables (AED, DR, FS, MPI, PNFWTWI, WRAL and D_i) were independent variables. This equation was estimated to analyse which of the poverty determinant variables was significantly associated with rural poverty and also what was the contribution of irrigation (GIV, CIV, and TIV) in reducing rural poverty compared to rainfed area.

3.6. Limitation of the Study

The major limitations of the study are as follows:

1. Among the major States, only 14 States were taken for the

State-level study in India. The results of the study may vary if more States were to be included in the analysis.

2. Due to non-availability of comparable district-wise poverty and other related data for all the districts of India, only 178 districts from 13 States were selected for the study.
3. It was carried out only in four villages of Aranthangi taluk in Pudukkottai district of Tamil Nadu in India. Other villages were not included for study due to resource and time constraints. Therefore, the results of the study can be used only with similar environment.
4. Agricultural labourers (landless labourers) alone were selected as sample respondents from the sample villages because majority of poor people were from agricultural wage labour households. Therefore, the results of the study can be applied only to agricultural labour households.

4
Study Area

4.1. Introduction

There are mainly three types of irrigation sources such as well, canal and tank. Therefore, three villages were selected on the basis of irrigation sources to study the relationship between sources-wise irrigation and rural poverty. Another village was selected as a sample of rainfed area for the purpose of comparison. Thus, a total of four villages were selected for the field based sample survey. In this chapter, a detailed profile of the study area is presented to explain the overall agro-economic characteristics of the selected villages and the study area.

4.2. Background

India is one of the fast developing countries in the world. It is the seventh largest country by area with 32,87,263 sq. kms., which is 2.42 per cent of the world area. It is the second most populous country with over 121.02 crore people, which is 17.5 per cent of World population (Census of India, 2011) and the most populous democracy in the world. India borders on China, Nepal and Bhutan in the north, Myanmar, and Bangladesh in the east and Pakistan and Afghanistan in the west. Arabian Sea is in the west, Indian Ocean in the south and Bay of Bengal in its east of India. The cultivable area is 141.23 million hectares (43% of total area) and the forest area is about 6,92,027 sq. kms. (21.05% of the total geographical area). The net sown area is 142 million hectares of which area under foodgrain is 125 million hectares (75.75% of net sown area) in 2013. Irrigated and rainfed area is 45% and 55% of net sown area respectively in the year 2013 (GoI, 2014). With 2.42 per cent of world area, India has 29 States, seven Union Territories, 640 districts, 5,925 sub-districts, 7,933 towns and 6,40,930 villages (Census of India, 2011).

The India Map 4.1 depicts the 14 major States which were selected for the analysis. The impact of irrigation on rural poverty across States in India was analysed by taking 14 major States as the sample. As mentioned in the first chapter, one of the objectives of the study was to analyse the impact of irrigation on rural poverty reduction across districts of various States in India. Therefore, 178 districts were selected, only from 13 States in India, for the present study.

Among the 29 States of India, Tamil Nadu is one of the most developed States in India. Tamil Nadu is the 11th largest, seventh most populous and second most economically important State in Southern India. It is situated on the south-eastern side of the Indian Peninsula, with the Bay of Bengal in the east, the Indian Ocean in the south, and bounded by the States of Kerala and Karnataka in the west, and in the north by Andhra Pradesh and Karnataka. Bordered by the Bay of Bengal on its east, it has the second largest coastline in India, with a length of 1,076 kms. and it is an important centre for sea trade.

Tamil Nadu has 32 districts, 215 sub-districts, 1,097 towns and 15,979 villages as per the Census of India, 2011 (*see*, Map 4.2). Out of the 32 districts of Tamil Nadu, Pudukkottai is one of the backward districts in the State. Pudukkottai district was created out of Tiruchirappalli and Thanjavur districts in January 1974. The district has an area of 4663 sq. kms., with a coast line of 39 km. It is bounded by Tiruchirappalli in the north and west, Sivaganga district in the south, Bay of Bengal in the east and Thanjavur district in the north-east. At present, this district is composed of two revenue divisions, namely, Pudukkottai and Aranthangi with nine taluks, namely Kulathur, Illuppur, Alangudi, Pudukkottai, Gandarvakottai, Thirumayam, Aranthangi, Avudaiyrakoil and Manamelkudi (see, Map 4.3). There are 765 revenue villages in the district. Out of the 765 villages of Pudukkottai district, four villages were selected as the study area. These four villages are under Aranthangi taluk, which has 26 wards, 52 panchayat villages and 108 revenue villages. To study the source-wise impact of irrigation on rural poverty reduction, Ayangudi (GIV), Kalakudi (CIV), Kulattur (TIV) and Veeramangalam (RFV) were taken as sample villages (*see*, Map 4.4).

These villages were selected from Aranthangi taluk which is one of the taluks of Pudukkottai district in Tamil Nadu. Tamil Nadu

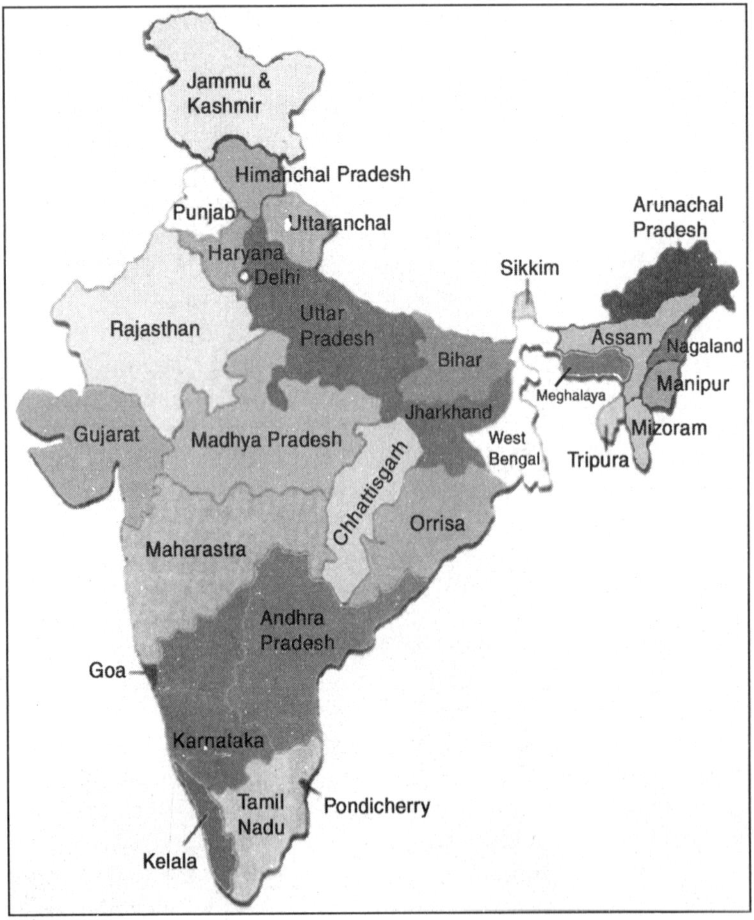

Map 4.1: Map of India

Map 4.2 displays the Pudukkottai district. Similarly, Pudukkottai district Map 4.3 displays the Aranthangi taluk. The four sample villages are shown in Aranthangi taluk map (see, Map 4.4). Finally, the consolidated map is presented in Map 4.5.

Ayangudi (Groundwater Irrigated Village) is a small village in Aranthangi taluk in Pudukkottai district of Tamil Nadu, India. It comes under Ayangudi panchayat. It is located 36 km. Towards south from district headquarters, Pudukkottai and 409 kms. from the State capital,

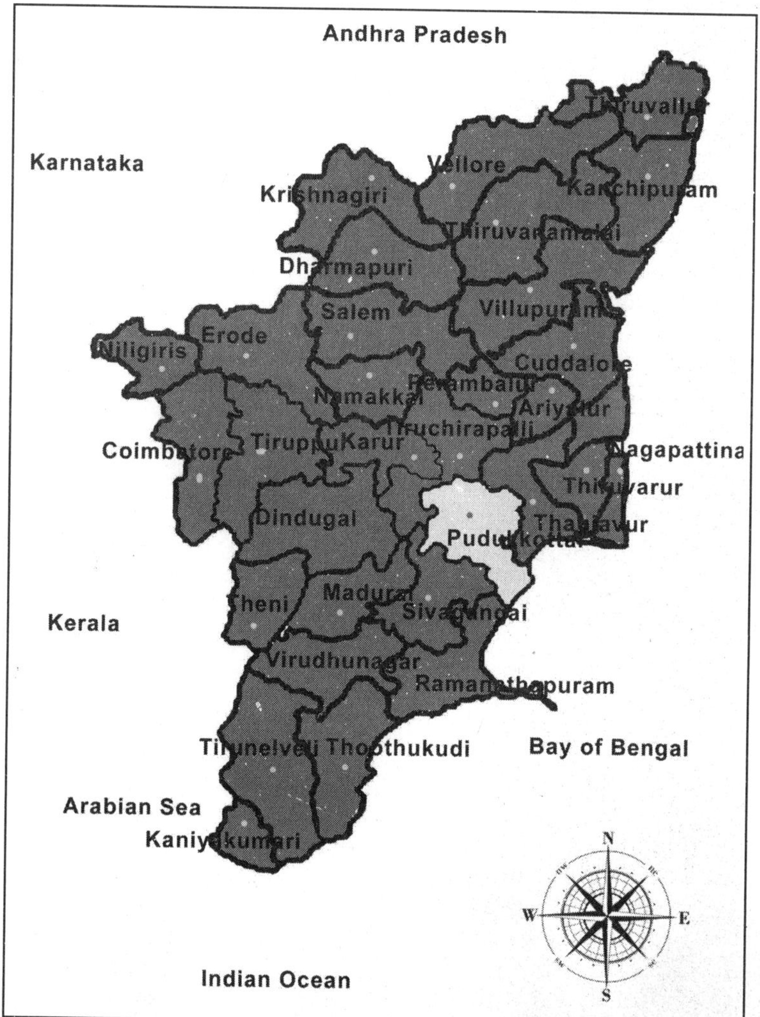

Map 4.2: Map of Tamil Nadu State

Chennai. It is surrounded by Avudaiyarkovil taluk towards south, Sakkottai taluk towards west, Arimalam taluk towards west and Thiruvarankulam taluk towards north. Karaikudi, Peravurani, Pudukkottai, Pattukkottai are the cities in the vicinity of Ayangudi. This place is on the border of the Pudukkottai and Sivaganga districts.

Likewise, Kalakudi (Canal Irrigated Village) is a small village in

Map 4.3: Map of Pudukkottai District

Aranthangi taluk in Pudukkottai district of Tamil Nadu, India. It comes under Kalakudi panchayat. It is located 36 km., towards south from district headquarters, Pudukkottai and 409 kms. from the State capital, Chennai. Kalakudi is surrounded by Avudaiyarkovil taluk towards south, Sakkottai taluk towards west, Arimalam taluk towards east and Thiruvarankulam taluk towards north. Karaikudi, Peravurani and Pattukkottai are the cities close to Kalakudi. This place is also on the border of the Pudukkottai and Sivaganga districts.

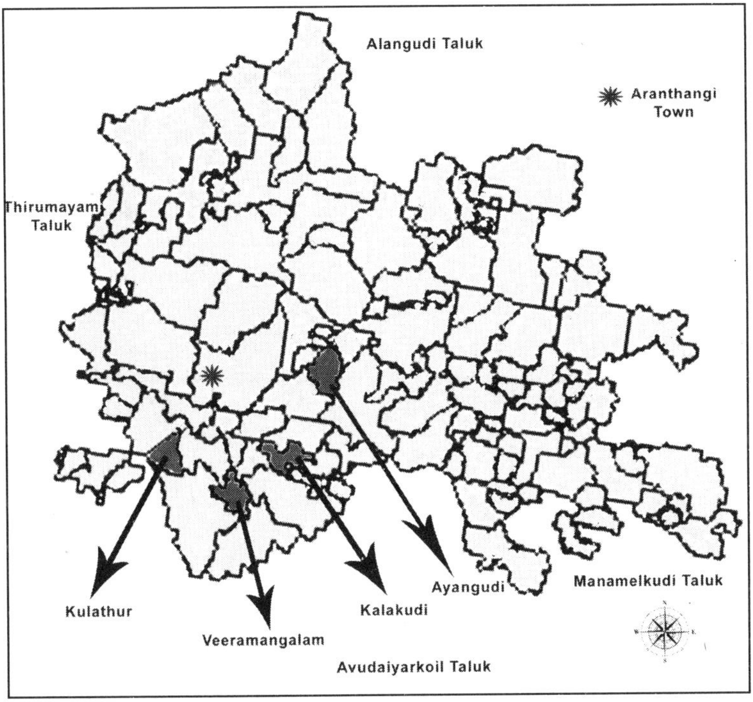

Map 4.4: Map of Aranthangi Taluk

Similarly, Kulattur (Tank Irrigated Village) is a small village in Aranthangi taluk in Pudukkottai district of Tamil Nadu, India. It comes under Paravakottai panchayat. It is located 25 kms. towards east from district headquarters, Pudukkottai and 394 kms. from the State capital, Chennai. Kulattur is surrounded by Aranthangi taluk towards south, Thiruvarankulam taluk and Pudukkottai taluk towards west and Peravurani taluk towards east. Pudukkottai, Peravurani, Karaikudi and Pattukkottai are the cities closer to Kulattur. This place is on the border of the Pudukkottai and Sivaganga districts.

Veeramangalam (Rainfed Village) is a village in Aranthangi in Pudukkottai district of Tamil Nadu, India. It is located 41 kms. towards south from district headquarters, Pudukkottai and 415 km. from State capital, Chennai. Avudaiyarkovil, Nagudi, Aranthangi, Rethinakottai and Aliyanilai are the villages closer to Veeramangalam. Veeramangalam is surrounded by Avudaiyarkovil taluk towards east, Sakkottai taluk towards west, Arimalam taluk towards north and

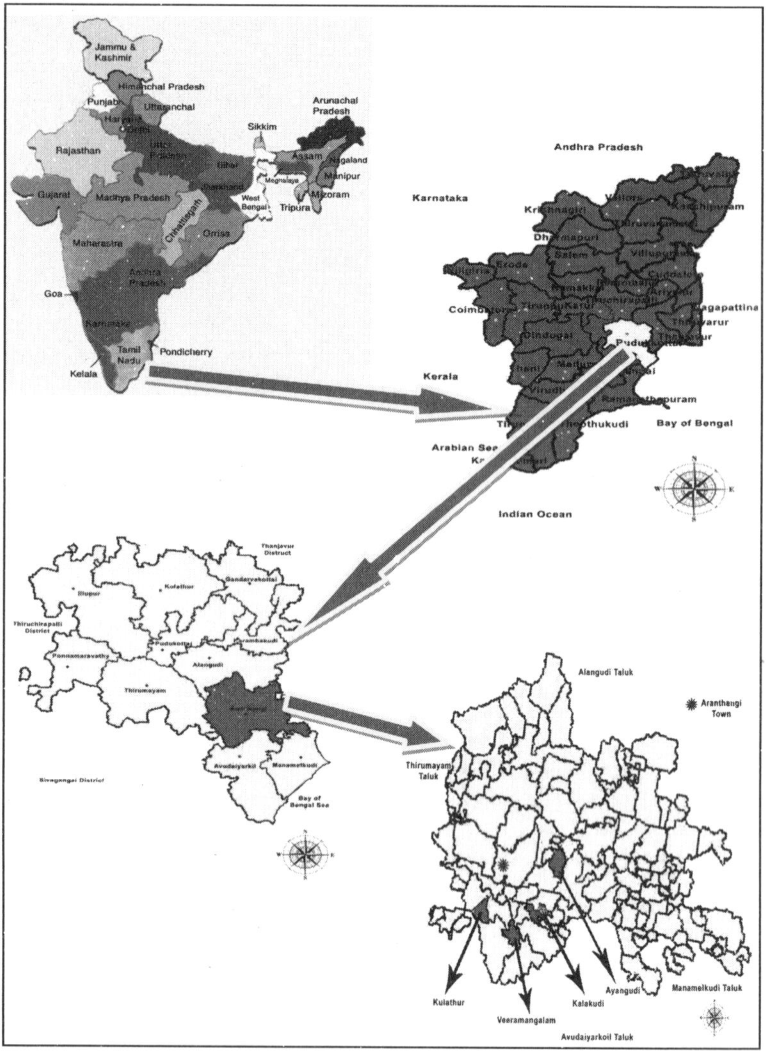

Map 4.5: Consolidated Maps of India, Tamil Nadu, Pudukkottai District and Aranthangi Taluk

Kannankudi taluk towards west. Karaikudi, Peravurani, Pudukkottai, Pattukkottai are the cities in the neighbourhood of Veeramangalam.

4.3. Climate

India is home to an extraordinary variety of climatic regions, ranging from tropical in the south to temperate and alpine in the Himalayan North where elevated regions receive sustained winter snowfall. The nation's climate is strongly influenced by the Himalayas and the Thar Desert. The Himalayas act as a barrier to the frigid katabolic winds flowing down from Central Asia, keeping the bulk of the Indian Subcontinent warmer than most locations at similar latitudes. The country is influenced by two seasons of rains, accompanied by seasonal reversal of winds from January to July. During the winters, dry and cold air, blowing from the northerly latitudes from a north-easterly direction, prevails over the Indian region.

Tamil Nadu is the southern State of India. The climate of Tamil Nadu is tropical in nature, with variation in summer and winter temperatures. While April-June is the hottest summer period, with the temperature rising up to the 40°C mark, November-February represent the coolest winter period, with temperature hovering around 20°C, making the climate quite pleasant. Tamil Nadu gets its maximum rains from the North-East Monsoon between October and December, when rest of the country remains dry. The average annual rainfalls in Tamil Nadu range between 25 and 75 inches (635 and 1905 mm) a year.

Pudukkottai district recorded the highest day temperature during summer which is between 30°C to 42°C. Average temperatures of January is 27°C, February is 27°C, March is 30°C, April is 33°C and May is 34°C. Climate plays a vital role in the development of the district. Rainfall and temperature are the two important climatic parameters which determine the climatic situation of any place. Pudukkottai is a semi-arid district, situated in the central part of Tamil Nadu. The highest rainfall is received during the north east monsoon in the southern and eastern parts of the district.

Aranthangi, one of the taluks in Pudukkottai district, is too hot during summer. The highest day temperature in Aranthangi during summer is between 29°C to 42°C. The four sample villages selected for the field study, namely Ayangudi, Kalakudi, Kulathur and Veeramangalam are situated 12 kms, 12 kms, 9 kms and 10 kms from Aranthangi respectively. Therefore, the climate of four villages is more or less equal to Aranthangi.

4.4. Land-Use Pattern

The density of population in India is 364 per sq. km. and that of

Tamil Nadu is 555 per sq. km., as per the Census of India, 2011. Likewise, the density of Pudukkottai district for 2011 is 348 per sq. km., the density of Aranthangi taluk is 88 per sq. km., and 324 per sq. km., 844 per sq. km.,152 per sq. km. and 159 per sq. km. are the density of GIV, CIV, TIV and RFV sample villages respectively (Census of India, 2011).

Table 4.1 shows the land-use pattern of the study area. Total geographical area is categorised into agricultural area, forest area, cropped area, irrigated area and un-irrigated area. The pattern of land-use in India is the same for Tamil Nadu and this pattern is applicable to the four villages under GIV, CIV, TIV and RFV as well. Out of the total geographical area in India, the forest area is 21.30 per cent, barren land is 5.19 per cent, cultivable waste land is 3.85 per cent and net sown area is 43.07 per cent in the year 2013. Similarly, in the case of Tamil Nadu, 16.34 per cent is forest area, 3.76 per cent is barren lands and 38.09 per cent is net sown area for the year 2013. Pudukkottai district has 5.05 per cent of forest area which is higher than the State forest areas. The net sown area of Pudukkottai district (32.03%) is nearer to the State net sown area. Aranthangi taluk has 2.44 per cent of forest area, 2.19 per cent of barren land, 1.10 per cent of cultivable waste land and net sown area is 42.05 per cent in 2013 (GoI, 2014). Net sown area of Aranthangi taluk is higher than that of the district and State net sown area. Out of the four villages, GIV recorded the highest net sown area (65.30%), followed by CIV (64.33%), TIV (50.50%) and RFV (30.80%). Reason for this is that GIV enjoyed reliable irrigation facilities, followed by CIV, TIV and RFV.

4.5. Irrigation Pattern

Land use pattern also includes the irrigated areas. As mentioned in the methodology chapter, there are three sources of irrigation, namely groundwater irrigation, canal irrigation and tank irrigation. According to Table 4.2, while groundwater irrigated area was 61.41 per cent and tank irrigated area was 3.15 per cent, the canal irrigated area was 24.63 per cent in the total irrigated area in India.

In the case of Tamil Nadu, groundwater irrigated area was 55.70 per cent, whereas tank irrigated area was 19.30 per cent in 2013 (GoI, 2014). This shows that groundwater irrigation source is the dominant source in India as well as in the State of Tamil Nadu. But, in

Table 4.1: Land-Use Pattern in 2013

(in hectares)

Land	*India*	*Tamil Nadu*	*Pudukkottai*	*Aranthangi*	*Ayangudi (GIV)*	*Kalakudi (CIV)*	*Kulattur (TIV)*	*Veeraman-galam (RFV)*
Total Geographical Area	328726000 (100)	13006000 (100)	466329 (100)	44756 (100)	944.25 (100)	191.03 (100)	358.06 (100)	1115.13 (100)
Forest	70006000 (21.30)	2125000 (16.34)	23535 (5.05)	1093 (2.44)	0 (0.00)	0 (0.00)	0.81 (0.23)	269.12 (24.13)
Barren and uncultivable lands	17051000 (5.19)	489000 (3.76)	9863 (2.12)	982 (2.19)	222.7 (23.58)	65.98 (34.54)	98.61 (27.54)	376.42 (33.76)
Land put to non-agricultural use	26513000 (8.07)	2177000 (16.74)	129844 (27.84)	13153 (29.39)	0 (0.00)	0 (0.00)	0 (0.00)	0 (0.00)
Cultivable waste	12657000 (3.85)	331000 (2.54)	9982 (2.14)	741 (1.66)	0 (0.00)	0 (0.00)	0.81 (0.23)	0 (0.00)
Permanent pastures and grazing land	10301000 (3.13)	110000 (0.85)	5124 (1.10)	151 (0.34)	0 (0.00)	1.03 (0.54)	73.9 (20.64)	18.35 (1.65)
Miscellaneous tree crops and groves	3207000 (0.98)	252000 (1.94)	27762 (5.95)	1826 (4.08)	0 (0.00)	0 (0.00)	2.17 (0.61)	7.22 (0.65)
Current fallows	14267000 (4.34)	1015000 (7.80)	11189 (2.40)	1718 (3.84)	104.91 (11.11)	0.17 (0.09)	0.81 (0.23)	15.75 (1.41)
Other than current fallows	10321000 (3.14)	1540000 (11.84)	92947 (19.93)	4867 (10.87)	0 (0.00)	0 (0.00)	0 (0.00)	84.85 (7.61)
Net sown area	141579000 (43.07)	4954000 (38.09)	149367 (32.03)	18819 (42.05)	616.64 (65.30)	122.89 (64.33)	180.81 (50.50)	343.42 (30.80)

Note: Figures in the brackets are percentage of the respective total geographical area.
Source: GoI (2013), Department of Agriculture, Aranthangi Taluk and Village Administrative Officers' Records (various villages).

Table 4.2: Irrigation Pattern in 2013

(in hectares)

Land	*India*	*Tamil Nadu*	*Pudukkottai*	*Aranthangi*	*Ayangudi (GIV)*	*Kalakudi (CIV)*	*Kulattur (TIV)*	*Veeraman-galam (RFV)*
Net Irrigated Area	63601000 (100)	2912000 (100)	110784 (100)	15620 (100)	611.69 (100)	64.12 (100)	90.81 (100)	0 (0.00)
Well Irrigated Area	39060000 (61.41)	1622000 (55.70)	31304 (28.26)	2339 (14.97)	355.8 (58.17)	0 (0.00)	0 (0.00)	0 (0.00)
Canal Irrigated Area	15667000 (24.63)	474000 (16.28)	5532 (4.99)	2253 (14.42)	255.89 (41.83)	64.12 (100)	0 (0.00)	0 (0.00)
Tank Irrigated Area	2004000 (3.15)	533000 (18.30)	73948 (66.75)	11028 (70.60)	0 (0.00)	0 (0.00)	90.81 (100)	0 (0.00)
Other Irrigated Area	6871000 (10.80)	283000 (9.72)	0 (0.00)	0 (0.00)	0 (0.00)	0 (0.00)	0 (0.00)	0 (0.00)
Rainfed Area	77978000 (55.07)	2042000 (41.22)	38583 (25.83)	3199 (17.00)	4.94 (0.80)	58.77 (47.82)	90.00 (49.78)	343.42 (100)

Note: Figures in the brackets are percentage of the respective net irrigated areas and net sown areas (for rainfed areas).

Source: Same as in Table 4.1.

Pudukkottai district and Aranthangi taluk, tank irrigated area accounted for major share followed by groundwater irrigated area and canal irrigated area. Similarly, GIV represented 58.17 per cent of groundwater irrigated area which was the highest as compared to other sources of irrigation. CIV recorded 100 per cent canal irrigated area which was the highest among other irrigated areas, TIV recorded 100 per cent tank irrigated area which was the highest among other irrigated areas in the year 2013.

4.6. Cropping Pattern

India practices diversified cropping pattern, which is also true in the case of sample villages. Table 4.3 shows the area under some of the major crops, cultivated in the study area. Area under paddy in India is 30.99 per cent, Tamil Nadu is 38.47 per cent, Pudukkottai is 62.20 per cent, Aranthangi is 71.79 per cent, Ayangudi is 41.91 per cent, Kalakudi is 68.45 per cent, Kulattur is 61.95 per cent and Veeramangalam is 80.19 per cent during 2013-14. This shows that among the crops referred to in Table 4.3, area under paddy was the highest not only in India but also in all the four sample villages. Out of the four villages, Veeramangalam recorded the highest area under paddy cultivation, followed by Kalakudi, Kulattur and Ayangudi. Area under pulses comes next to the paddy cultivated area in India and Tamil Nadu State. But area under groundnut comes next to the paddy in Pudukkottai district and Aranthangi taluk. Ayangudi village has 41.41 per cent of area under coconut which is next to the paddy cultivated area during 2013-14. Similarly, mango in Kalakudi and Kulattur and coconut in Veeramangalam, came next to paddy during the same period. On the whole, both foodgrain crop and cash crop were found in Ayangudi village but not in other villages. This shows that irrigation helped to increase diversified cropping pattern.

4.7. Characteristics of Study Area

According to the Census of 2011, the total number of households of India was 249.45 million, of which Tamil Nadu had a share of 18.52 million. Pudukkottai, one of the districts of Tamil Nadu contained 3,87,679 households. Similarly, Aranthangi recorded 9690, Ayangudi, 835, Kalakudi, 410, Kulattur, 136 and Veeramangalam, 419. The sex-ratio in India, which was 933 in 2001, had increased by 10 to 943 in

Table 4.3: Cropping Pattern During 2013-14

(in hectares)

Crops	*India*	*Tamil Tadu*	*Pudukkottai*	*Aranthangi*	*Ayangudi (GIV)*	*Kalakudi (CIV)*	*Kulattur (TIV)*	*Veeramangalam (RFV)*
Paddy	43870000 (30.99)	1906000 (38.47)	92901 (62.20)	13510 (71.79)	258.42 (41.91)	84.12 (68.45)	112.01 (61.95)	275.42 (80.19)
Sugarcane	5287000 (3.73)	316000 (6.38)	7858 (5.26)	780 (4.14)	24.04 (3.90)	0 (0.00)	1.6 (0.88)	0 (0.00)
Pulses	25750000 (18.19)	637000 (12.86)	1754 (1.17)	140 (0.74)	49 (7.95)	0 (0.00)	0 (0.00)	0 (0.00)
Cashew	589000 (0.42)	97000 (1.96)	8620 (5.77)	380 (2.02)	0 (0.00)	0 (0.00)	5 (2.77)	0 (0.00)
Coconut	1839000 (1.30)	410000 (8.28)	8214 (5.50)	1800 (9.56)	255.36 (41.41)	2.07 (1.08)	2.17 (1.20)	7.25 (2.11)
Turmeric	198000 (0.14)	51000 (1.03)	8 (0.54)	3 (0.02)	0 (0.00)	0 (0.00)	0 (0.00)	0 (0.00)
Mango	1358000 (0.96)	139000 (2.81)	800 (0.54)	114 (0.61)	0.16 (0.03)	5 (2.62)	5 (2.77)	1 (0.29)
Banana	562000 (0.40)	107000 (2.16)	2955 (1.98)	108 (0.57)	0.85 (0.41)	5 (2.62)	0 (0.00)	0 (0.00)
Tapioca	216000 (0.15)	120000 (2.42)	49 (0.03)	13 (0.07)	0 (0.00)	1 (0.52)	0 (0.00)	0 (0.00)
Maize	8392000 (5.93)	230000 (4.64)	2888 (1.93)	314 (1.67)	0 (0.00)	0 (0.00)	0 (0.00)	0 (0.00)
Others	95779000 (27.11)	981000 (3.67)	7232 (4.23)	21 (0.11)	28.81 (4.67)	113.84 (59.59)	55.03 (30.44)	59.77 (17.40)
Net sown area	141579000 (100)	4954000 (100)	149367 (100)	18819 (100)	616.64 (100)	122.89 (100)	180.81 (100)	343.42 (0.00)

Note: Figures in the brackets are percentage of the respective gross sown areas.
Source: Same as in Table 4.1.

2011. In rural areas, the sex-ratio had increased from 946 to 949. The corresponding increase in urban areas was 29 points from 900 to 929. Likewise, the sex-ratio of Tamil Nadu, which was 987 in 2001, had increased by 9 to 996 in 2011.

In rural areas, the sex-ratio had increased from 992 to 993. The corresponding increase in urban areas was 18 points from 982 to 1000. Regarding sex-ratio in Pudukkottai district, it stood at 1015 per 1000 males. The Aranthangi taluk represented of sex-ratio of 1028. It has been observed that out of four sample villages of Aranthangi taluk, Kalakudi recorded the highest sex-ratio, followed by Veeramangalam, Kulathur and Ayangudi. All the villages recorded a sex-ratio above the national average sex-ratio of 942.75 (see, Table 4.4).

The average national child sex-ratio in India was 919 of which rural child sex-ratio was 923 and urban child sex-ratio was 905. Tamil Nadu child sex-ratio was 943, higher than the national. Child sex-ratio of Pudukkottai district was 959 as per 2011 Census data. In rural and urban areas of Pudukkottai district, child sex-ratio was 963 and 943 females per 1000 males respectively. The Kalakudi village recorded the highest child sex-ratio (1616) and Kulattur recorded the lowest child sex-ratio (793).

As per the Census 2011, the total population of India was 1210.57 million, in which the rural population was 833.46 million (68.85% of total population) and the urban population was 377.12 million (31.15% of total population). The total population of Tami Nadu was 72.15 million, including rural population of 37.22 million (51.60% of total population) and urban population of 34.92 million which is 48.40 per cent of total population (see, Table 4.5).

Pudukkottai recorded a population of 1,618,345 of which male and female were 803,188 (50.09% of district's population) and 815,157 (49.63% of district's population) respectively. Out of the total Pudukkottai population, 2011 Census reported that 19.55 per cent lived in urban regions and 80.45 per cent lived in rural region of the district. In total, 13,01,991 people lived in rural areas of which males were 6, 45,505 and females were 6,56,486. Among the four selected villages, Kulattur represented the highest male population of 49.54 per cent, whereas Kalakudi recorded the highest female population of 54.62 per cent in the total population of respective villages. With regard to male and female population, the proportion of female was higher in Aranthangi taluk of Pudukottai district (see, Table 4.5).

Table 4.4: Demography of Study Area in 2011

Particulars		*India*	*Tamil Nadu*	*Pudukkottai*	*Aranthangi*	*Ayangudi (GIV)*	*Kalakudi (CIV)*	*Kulattur (TIV)*	*Veeramangalam (RFV)*
No. of HHs	Total	249454252	18524982	387679	96900	835	410	136	419
	Rural	168565486	9528495	310285	NIL	835	410	136	419
	Urban	80888766	8996487	77394	9690	NIL	NIL	NIL	NIL
Family Size (Average)	Total	4.85	3.89	4.17	4.03	3.50	3.93	4.02	4.25
	Rural	4.94	3.91	4.20	NIL	3.50	3.93	4.02	4.25
	Urban	4.66	3.88	4.09	4.03	NIL	NIL	NIL	NIL
Sex ratio (%)	Total	942.75	996.43	1014.90	1028.79	1099.93	1203.55	1018.45	1139.26
	Rural	949.02	993.12	1017.01	0.00	1099.93	1203.55	1018.45	1139.26
	Urban	929.04	999.98	1006.27	1028.79	NIL	NIL	NIL	NIL
Child Sex Ratio (%)	Total	918.50	943.27	959.61	980.13	1041.92	1616.44	793.10	1100.00
	Rural	923.20	935.76	963.39	NIL	1041.92	1616.44	793.10	1100.00
	Urban	905.45	951.70	943.36	980.13	NIL	NIL	NIL	NIL

Source: Census of India (2011).

Child population means the population in the age group of 0-6 years. As per the Census of India (2011), child population was 164.48 million, which was 13.59 per cent of the total population, out of which 121.28 million (14.55%) were from rural areas and 43.19 million (11.45%) were from the urban areas. But, in the case of Tamil Nadu, child population was 7.42 million (10.29% of total State population), including 3.91 million (10.51% of total State population) from rural areas and 3.51 million (10.06 per cent of total State population) from urban areas. Compared to the Census of India (2001), the child population had increased by 1.90 million in the State. In terms of proportion of child population to the total population, there was a decline of 1.6 per cent in rural areas and 0.90 per cent in urban areas in Tamil Nadu (*see*, Table 4.6). Pudukkottai recorded a child population of 1,79,688, which was 11.10 per cent of total district population. The male child population was 91,696 (11.42%) and female child population was 87,992 (10.79%) in Pudukkottai district. The child population in the rural area was 11.22 per cent and it was 10.64 per cent in the urban population in Pudukkottai district. Similarly, Aranthangi recorded 10.72 per cent of child population. 11.67 per cent, 11.84 per cent, 9.51 per cent and 12.96 per cent were recorded against Ayangudi, Kalakudi, Kulattur and Veeramangalam respectively. It implies that Veeramangalam possessed the highest child population among the four villages. This means dependency ratio in Veeramagalam village (RFV) was the highest among four villages.

The total Scheduled Caste (SC) population in Census 2011 was 201.38 million (16.63%) in India. The SC population constituted 153.85 million in rural areas and 47.53 million in urban areas. The total Scheduled Caste (SC) population in Tamil Nadu was 14.38 million (20%). Out of 4.96 million, 9.47 million (25%) were from rural areas and 4.91 million (14.21%) from urban areas. In fact, Pudukkotai district recorded 2,84,804 (17.60%) of SC population, with 2,46,531 (18.93%) in rural areas and 38,273 (12.10%) in urban areas. Female SC population was 5.54 per cent, Male SC population was 5.97 per cent and total SC population was 5.75 per cent in Aranthangi taluk. Kulattur recorded the highest SC population (50.09%), followed by Veeramangalam, Kalakudi and Ayangudi (see, Table 4.7).

According to the Census Report 2011, Scheduled Tribe (ST) population was 104.28 million, which was 8.61 per cent of total

Table 4.5: Population Rate of Study Area in 2011

(per cent)

Study Area	Total			Rural			Urban		
	Person	Male	Female	Person	Male	Female	Person	Male	Female
India	100.00	51.47	48.53	68.85	68.63	69.08	31.15	31.37	30.92
Tamil Nadu	100.00	50.09	49.91	51.60	51.69	51.52	48.40	48.31	48.48
Pudukkottai	100.00	49.63	50.37	80.45	80.37	80.53	19.55	19.63	19.47
Aranthangi	100.00	49.29	50.71	NIL	NIL	NIL	100.00	49.29	50.71
Ayangudi (GIV)	100.00	47.62	52.38	100.00	47.62	52.38	NIL	NIL	NIL
Kalakkudi (CIV)	100.00	45.38	54.62	100.00	45.38	54.62	NIL	NIL	NIL
Kulattur (TIV)	100.00	49.54	50.46	100.00	49.54	50.46	NIL	NIL	NIL
Veeramangalam (RFV)	100.00	46.75	53.25	100.00	46.75	53.25	NIL	NIL	NIL

Source: Same as in Table 4.4.

Table 4.6: Child Population Ratio of Study Area in 2011

(per cent)

Study Area	*Total*			*Rural*			*Urban*		
	Person	*Male*	*Female*	*Person*	*Male*	*Female*	*Person*	*Male*	*Female*
India	13.59	13.76	13.40	14.55	14.75	14.35	11.45	11.60	11.30
Tamil Nadu	10.29	10.57	10.01	10.51	10.82	10.19	10.06	10.31	9.81
Pudukkottai	11.10	11.42	10.79	11.22	11.52	10.91	10.64	10.98	10.30
Aranthangi	10.72	10.99	10.47	NIL	NIL	NIL	10.72	10.99	10.47
Ayangudi (GIV)	11.67	12.01	11.37	11.67	12.01	11.37	NIL	NIL	NIL
Kalakkudi (CIV)	11.84	9.97	13.39	11.84	9.97	13.39	NIL	NIL	NIL
Kulattur (TIV)	9.51	10.70	8.33	9.51	10.70	8.33	NIL	NIL	NIL
Veera-mangalam (RFV)	12.96	13.21	12.75	12.96	13.21	12.75	NIL	NIL	NIL

Source: Same as in Table 4.4.

population in India. ST population in rural India was 93.81 million (11.26% of total ST population) and the ST population of urban area was 10.46 million (11.26% of total ST population). In terms of proportion, the ST population constituted 8.61 per cent of the total population. Correspondingly, in Tamil Nadu, ST population was 7.94 lakh (1.10%) of which 6.61 lakh were in rural areas and 1.34 lakh were in urban areas. In terms of proportion, the ST population constituted 0.08 per cent of the total population in Pudukottai district and 0.78% in Aranthangi taluk. However, there was no ST population in the four selected villages (*see*, Table 4.8).

Education is the major factor for economic development as well as human development. The literacy is measured in the age group of seven years and above. According to the Census of India (2011), the number of literates in India was 763.49 million which was 72.99 per cent of total population in the age group of seven and above years and illiterates were 447.07 million (27.01%) in India. Out of an increase of 202.89 million literates during the decade 2001-11, rural areas accounted for 482.65 million (67.77%) and urban areas accounted for 280.85 million (84.11%). About 73.54 per cent and 87.04 per cent of total literates of Tamil Nadu were in rural and urban areas respectively. Average literacy rate in Pudukkottai district was 77.19 per cent, of which males and females were 85.56 per cent and 69.00 per cent literates respectively. The number of literates in Aranthangi taluk was 31,491 (90.37%). The highest literacy rate was recorded in Kalakudi (88.82%), and Kulattur (64.44%) recorded the lowest literacy rate, out of the four sample villages in Aranthangi taluk (*see*, Table 4.9).

Employment growth in the organised sector, public and private, had increased by 1.0 per cent in 2011, which was lower than the annual growth for 2001. The annual growth rate for private sector was much higher than that for public sector. The share of women in organised sector employment was 20.50 per cent during 2009-11 and it remained nearly constant in recent years. Only 15.60 per cent of the total workforce were regular wage earners or salaried, while 33.50 per cent were casual labour and 51 per cent were self-employed during 2011-12. The work force registered a growth of 19.81 per cent, which was marginally higher than the overall population growth rate of 17.70 per cent during the decade. The Work Participation Rate (WPR) for the country worked out to 39.82 per cent. This was marginally higher than the corresponding WPR of 39.1 per cent in Census 2001. The

Table 4.7: Scheduled Caste Population Rate of Study Area in 2011

(in per cent)

Study Area	*Total*			*Rural*			*Urban*		
	Person	*Male*	*Female*	*Person*	*Male*	*Female*	*Person*	*Male*	*Female*
India	16.63	16.62	16.66	18.46	18.50	18.41	12.60	12.49	12.72
Tamil Nadu	20.01	19.94	20.09	25.45	25.35	25.55	14.21	14.14	14.29
Pudukkottai	17.60	17.61	17.59	18.93	18.93	18.94	12.10	10.98	10.30
Aranthangi	5.75	5.97	5.54	NIL	NIL	NIL	5.75	5.97	5.54
Ayangudi (GIV)	6.20	6.18	6.21	6.20	6.18	6.21	NIL	NIL	NIL
Kalakkudi (CIV)	12.77	11.89	13.51	12.77	11.89	13.51	NIL	NIL	NIL
Kulattur (TIV)	50.09	49.45	50.72	50.09	49.45	50.72	NIL	NIL	NIL
Veeramangalam (RFV)	26.99	28.21	25.92	26.99	28.21	25.92	NIL	NIL	NIL

Source: Same as in Table 4.4.

Table 4.8: Scheduled Tribe Population Rate of Study Area in 2011

(in per cent)

Study Area	*Total*			*Rural*			*Urban*		
	Person	*Male*	*Female*	*Person*	*Male*	*Female*	*Person*	*Male*	*Female*
India	8.61	8.41	8.83	11.26	11.02	11.51	2.77	2.70	2.85
Tamil Nadu	1.10	1.11	1.09	1.77	1.78	1.76	0.38	0.39	0.38
Pudukkottai	0.08	0.08	0.08	0.06	0.06	0.06	0.14	0.15	0.14
Aranthangi	0.79	0.81	0.77	NIL	NIL	NIL	0.79	0.81	0.77
Ayangudi (GIV)	NIL	NIL	NIL	NIL	NIL	NIL	NIL	NIL	NIL
Kalakkudi (CIV)	NIL	NIL	NIL	NIL	NIL	NIL	NIL	NIL	NIL
Kulattur (TIV)	NIL	NIL	NIL	NIL	NIL	NIL	NIL	NIL	NIL
Veeramangalam (RFV)	NIL	NIL	NIL	NIL	NIL	NIL	NIL	NIL	NIL

Source: Same as in Table 4.4.

Table 4.9: Literacy Rate of Study Area in 2011

(*in per cent*)

Study Area	*Total*			*Rural*			*Urban*		
	Person	*Male*	*Female*	*Person*	*Male*	*Female*	*Person*	*Male*	*Female*
India	72.99	80.89	64.64	67.77	77.15	57.93	84.11	88.76	79.11
Tamil Nadu	80.09	86.77	73.44	73.54	82.04	65.05	87.04	91.80	82.31
Pudukkottai	77.19	85.56	69.00	74.37	83.53	65.42	88.74	93.84	83.71
Aranthangi	90.37	94.90	85.99	NIL	NIL	NIL	90.37	94.90	85.99
Ayangudi (GIV)	80.08	89.22	71.83	80.08	89.22	71.83	NIL	NIL	NIL
Kalakkudi (CIV)	88.82	95.14	83.36	88.82	95.14	83.36	NIL	NIL	NIL
Kulattur (TIV)	64.44	81.40	48.22	64.44	81.40	48.22	NIL	NIL	NIL
Veeramangalam (RFV)	78.27	87.69	70.05	78.27	87.69	70.05	NIL	NIL	NIL

Source: Same as in Table 4.4.

WPR for males had reduced marginally to 25.51 per cent in 2011 from 25.62 per cent in Census 2001. The percentage of main workers among the male workers was 82.30 per cent and female workers, 59.62 per cent, in Census 2011.

The Census 2011 report shows that the total number of workers in India was 481.74 million (39.79% of total population). Out of the total working population, 331.86 million (53.26%) workers were male and 149.88 million (25.51%) workers were female. It is also pointed out that the rural workers were 348.59 million (41.83% of rural population) and urban workers were 133.15 million (35.31% of rural population) in India. The working population of Tamil Nadu was 32.89 million that represented 45.58 per cent of total working population of India. Similarly, 21.43 million (59.31%) workers were males and 11.44 million (31.80%) were females. Out of the increase of five million workers during the decade 2001-11, male workers had accounted for 3.30 million and female workers 1.71 million and 18.86 million (50.66%) and 140.23 lakhs (40.16%) workers were from rural and urban areas of Tamil Nadu respectively. The male workers in rural and urban areas were 11.21 (60.04%) and 10.22 (58.54%) million respectively. The female workers in rural and urban areas were7.64 (41.22%) and 3.80 lakh (21.78%) respectively.

The total working population of Pudukkottai district was 7.61 lakh (47.07%) of which 4.71 lakh (58.65%) were male and 2.90 lakh (35.65%) were female. Number of workers in Aranthangi taluk was 12,497 (32.02%). Out of four villages selected, the total number of workers in Ayangudi was 1620 (55.46%) of which 887 (63.77%) were male and 733 (47.91%) were female. Similarly, in Kalakudi, 683 (42.34%) constituted the number of working population, including 441 (60.25%) male and 242 (27.47%) female working population. Kulattur recorded 268 (48.99%) working population and 175 (64.58%) and 93 (33.70%) were the male and female working population in Kulattur Village respectively. Veeramangalam was a dry area, with 810 (45.45%) working population, of which, male and female were 470 (56.42%) and 340 (35.83%) working population respectively. It is found that Kulattur recorded the highest percentage of male working population, whereas the female workers were the highest in Ayangudi village (see, Table 4.10).

The total workers of India are divided into four sub-groups, namely main workers, marginal workers (3-6 months), marginal workers (0-3 months) and non-workers. For the first time in the Census of India (2011), marginal workers who worked for less than six months in the reference year, were further sub-divided in two categories, namely those who worked for less than 3 months and those who worked for 3 months or more, but less than six months. Each sub-group was categorised according to the economic activities of the workers into four categories such as Cultivators (CL), Agricultural Labourers (AL), working in Household Industries (HHI) and Other Workers (OW). Cultivators and agricultural labourers were engaged in the agricultural sector, except those engaged in plantation activities and others were considered as a part of other workers. About one-in-two males and two of every three females were engaged in agricultural activities either as a cultivator or agricultural labourer. The remaining workers were found in household industries and the rest of them were other workers.

Unemployment is one of the main factors that affect poverty reduction in India. The number of unemployed persons or non-working population was 728.82 million (60.21%) of which, male were 291.25 (46.74%) million and 437.57 million (74.49%) were female in India. The non-working population of rural and urban areas was 484.86 million (58.17%) and 243.96 million (64.69%). In fact, the non-working population of Tamil Nadu was 39.26 million (54.42%), including 18.36 (49.34%) and 20.89 (59.84%) million of rural and urban respectively (see, Table 4.11). Similarly, Pudukkottai district recorded 8.56 (52.93%) lakh as non-working population. The non-working population in Aranthangi taluk was 26537 (67.98%). The non-working population of Ayangudi, Kalakudi, Kulattur and Veeramangalam villages were respectively 1,301 (44.54%), 930 (57.66%), 279 (51.01%) and 972 (54.55%) respectively. Unemployment was the highest in Veeramangalam village compared to other villages. However, percentage of non-working population in all the selected villages was less than the national average and more than the State average. Hence, it is evident that Veeramangalam village, which is under rainfed area, should have more poor people than other villages.

4.8. Poverty Ratio

With reference to poverty ratio, the percentage of population below the poverty line in rainfed village (Veeramanagalam) was two times higher (63.98%) than the national rural poverty ratio (25.70%) and

Table 4.10: Employment Rate of Study Area in 2011

(in per cent)

Study Area	*Total*			*Rural*			*Urban*		
	Person	*Male*	*Female*	*Person*	*Male*	*Female*	*Person*	*Male*	*Female*
India	39.79	53.26	25.51	41.83	53.03	30.02	35.31	53.76	15.44
Tamil Nadu	45.58	59.31	31.80	50.66	60.04	41.22	40.16	58.54	21.78
Pudukkottai	47.07	58.65	35.65	49.88	59.53	40.38	35.49	55.05	16.06
Aranthangi	32.02	54.07	10.57	NIL	NIL	NIL	32.02	54.07	10.57
Ayangudi (GIV)	55.46	63.77	47.91	55.46	63.77	47.91	NIL	NIL	NIL
Kalakkudi (CIV)	42.34	60.25	27.47	42.34	60.25	27.47	NIL	NIL	NIL
Kulattur (TIV)	48.99	64.58	33.70	48.99	64.58	33.70	NIL	NIL	NIL
Veeramangalam (RFV)	45.45	56.42	35.83	45.45	56.42	35.83	NIL	NIL	NIL

Source: Same as in Table 4.4.

Table 4.11: Unemployment Rate of Study Area in 2011

(*in per cent*)

Study Area	*Total*			*Rural*			*Urban*		
	Person	*Male*	*Female*	*Person*	*Male*	*Female*	*Person*	*Male*	*Female*
India	60.21	46.74	74.49	58.17	46.97	69.98	64.69	46.24	84.56
Tamil Nadu	54.42	40.69	68.20	49.34	39.96	58.78	59.84	41.46	78.22
Pudukkottai	52.93	41.35	64.35	50.12	40.47	59.62	64.51	44.95	83.94
Aranthangi	67.98	45.93	89.43	NIL	NIL	NIL	67.98	45.93	89.43
Ayangudi (GIV)	44.54	36.23	52.09	44.54	36.23	52.09	NIL	NIL	NIL
Kalakkudi (CIV)	57.66	39.75	72.53	57.66	39.75	72.53	NIL	NIL	NIL
Kulattur (TIV)	51.01	35.42	66.30	51.01	35.42	66.30	NIL	NIL	NIL
Veeramangalam (RFV)	54.55	43.58	64.17	54.55	43.58	64.17	NIL	NIL	NIL

Source: Same as in Table 4.4.

four times higher than the State rural poverty ratio (15.83%) and district rural poverty ratio (18.60%). Similar results were also found in tank irrigated village (Kulattur). However, in the case of groundwater irrigated village, the poverty ratio was less than the national poverty ratio and more or less equal with the State and district poverty ratio (see, Table 4.12). This result shows that groundwater irrigation was more pronounced in determining rural poverty comparatively.

Table 4.12: Poverty Ratio of Study Area during 2011-12

(*in per cent*)

Study Area	*All India*	*Rural*	*Urban*
India	21.92	25.70	13.70
Tamil Nadu	11.28	15.83	6.54
Pudukkottai	23.65	18.60	28.70
Aranthangi	34.52	NA	34.52
Ayangudi (GIV)	17.16	17.16	NA
Kalakkudi (CIV)	37.16	37.16	NA
Kulattur (TIV)	53.78	53.78	NA
Veeramangalam (RFV)	63.98	63.98	NA

Source: Planning Commission (2014) and Deputy Director of Statistics, Pudukkottai (2013).

4.9. Conclusion

Demographic and socio-economic conditions of the study areas were analysed in this chapter to understand its development parameters. In conclusion, though the Tamil Nadu is one of the developed States in India, Pudukkottai remains a backward district in Tamil Nadu. All the three major sources of irrigated areas such as groundwater irrigated areas, canal irrigated areas, tank irrigated areas as well as rainfed areas are found in one of the taluks called Aranthangi in Pudukkottai district. Hence, Podukkottai district was selected as the study area for the detailed analysis.

5

Impact of Irrigation on Rural Poverty

A State Level Analysis

5.1. Introduction

Irrigation plays a vital role in the agricultural development in India and it is borne out by various studies (Bardhan, 1973; Dhawan, 1988; Rath and Mitra, 1989; Vaidyanathan *et al.*, 1994; Narayanamoorthy and Deshpande, 2003; Bhattarai *et al.*, 2007; Ghosh and Kumar, 2010). Similarly, agriculture is the major factor for rural poverty reduction (Ahluwalia, 1978; Ghosh, 1993, 1998; Fan *et al.*, 1999; Mellor, 2001; Narayanamoorthy, 2001; Hussain *et al.*, 2007; Thorat and Fan, 2007; Pandey and Reddy, 2012). Irrigation is also an important factor for rural poverty reduction which is also documented by quite a few studies (Narayanamoorthy, 2001; Bhattarai and Narayanamoorthy, 2003; Hussain and Hanjra, 2003, 2004; Shah and Singh, 2004; Hussain, 2007c; Narayanamoorthy, 2007; Narayanamoorthy and Hanjra, 2010; Ghosh, *et al.*, 2011, 2012). The impact of irrigation on poverty can be perceived through three different routes. First, the increased local availability and the resultant affordability of foodgrains due to lower prices reduced the number of poor people. Second, the increased labour absorption due to intensification of agriculture and consequent rise in wage rates and income, make it possible for the rural poor to cross the poverty barriers. Third, the secondary effects of irrigation in terms of increased service opportunities within and outside the rural areas, better quality of life and consequent industrialisation increased the tempo of economic activities in the irrigated regions, which resulted in poverty reduction (Narayanamoorthy, 2001).

Although irrigation has been recognised as a crucial factor in explaining the growth of agriculture and rural economy in the literature, it has not been used as one of the principal explanatory variables in the poverty-related studies in India until 2001, when a study by Narayanamoorthy (2001) directly related the irrigation variable to the rural poverty through a simple regression analysis. The explanation of cross-section variations in rural poverty has all along been sought through agricultural growth (Ahluwalia, 1978), average value of agricultural output per hectare (Sundaram and Tendulkar, 1988) or through output per hectare (Datt and Ravallion, 1996; Ravallion and Datt, 1996). However, the use of irrigation as an explanatory variable has not been attempted by studies on rural poverty till the year 2001. After the publication of Narayanamoorthy (2001), quite a few studies have attempted to study the relationship between the irrigation development and rural poverty by using aggregated and disaggregated data in India and in South Asia (Saleth *et al.*, 2003; Bhattarai and Narayanamoorthy, 2003; Hussain and Hanjra, 2003, 2004; Lipton, 2007; Narayanamoorthy, 2007; Narayanamoorthy and Hanjra, 2010).

It has been well recognised by these studies that irrigation is one of the principal causative factors behind the temporal changes in agricultural growth and hence, directly using irrigation as an explanatory factor is necessary. However, the available studies on the irrigation-poverty nexus have certain limitations. First, in most cases, percentage of irrigated area to cropped area is used for the analysis, which does not capture the density of irrigation in relation to rural population. Second, irrigation has not been used as a lagged variable in the regression analysis, which is needed because irrigation cannot instantaneously impact on rural poverty. Third, most studies have used very old data covering the period only up to 1993-94, which does not capture the current reality. Fourth, studies covering all the major States, with all the eight time points of poverty data, namely 1973-74, 1977-78, 1983, 1987-88, 1993-94, 1999-2000, 2004-05 and 2011-12, are not available. Therefore, there is a need to study the poverty-irrigation relationship covering very recent data. Keeping this in view, an attempt has been made in this chapter to test the relationship between the incidence of rural poverty and the development of irrigation, across the major States in India.

In order to study the relationship between irrigation and rural poverty across State of India, 14 major States of India were selected for the analysis. The 14 major States altogether accounted for about 95 per cent of the total population below the poverty line in rural

India, both in the early seventies (1973-74) and now. As mentioned in the methodology chapter, both descriptive and regression analysis were used for the analysis. The variables used for analysis, including their overall averages etc., are presented in Table 5.1.

5.2. Description of the Variables Used for Analysis

There are so many poverty determinant variables. However, only six poverty determinant variables (CI, IAPTRP, FPHRP, GIAGCA, PFG, PRP, RWAL and SDAPHRP) were selected for this study. The reason behind the selection of these variables was that they would greatly influence the Percentage of Rural Poverty (PRP) across space and time. Therefore, the variable PRP was selected as the dependent variable in the analysis, which is expressed in terms of Percentage of Rural Poverty (PRP) while Percentage of Irrigated Area Per Thousand Rural Population (IAPTRP) was used as the independent variable. Another irrigation variable Percentage of Gross Irrigated Area to

Table 5.1: Variables used in the Study for Analysis

Variable	*Description of the Variables*	*Unit*	*1973-74*		*2011-12*	
			AVG	*SD*	*AVG*	*SD*
CI	Cropping Intensity	%	122.61	13.60	142.65	25.92
IAPTRP	Irrigated Area Per Thousand Rural Population	ha	90.33	71.45	160.75	128.35
FPHRP	Foodgrain Production Per Head Rural Population	kg.	281.23	161.22	455.01	459.98
GIAGCA	Percentage of Gross Irrigated Area to Gross Cropped Area	%	26.87	18.01	51.49	24.48
PFG	Productivity of Foodgrain	kg./ha	965.00	382.68	2334.21	974.69
PRP	Percentage of Rural Poverty	%	53.86	12.37	21.42	9.89
RWAL	Real Wage Rate of Agriculture Labourer at (1986-87 prices)	Rs./day	9.36	3.59	30.56	11.48
SDAPHRP	State Domestic Product of Agriculture Per Hear Rural Population at (1986-87 prices)	Rs.	892.86	347.43	1500.41	749.68

Notes: SD—Standard Deviation; AVG—Average; ha—Hectare; kg—Kilogram.
Sources: GoI (various years) and Planning Commission (2014).

Gross Cropped Area (GIAGCA) was used in this analysis to understand the trends in irrigation development and poverty reduction from 1973-74 to 2011-12. Cropping Intensity (CI) is defined as the ratio of gross cropped area to net cropped area in percentage term and explains how intensively crops are cultivated in a year. Productivity of Foodgrain (PFG) was also used for this study. Other important indicators that would positively and directly influence the rural poverty are the Real Wage Rate of Agricultural Labourers (RWRAL), Foodgrain Production Per Head Rural Population (FPHRP) and State Domestic Product Per Head Rural Population (SDAPHRP) were used to study the incidence of poverty. These variables were also used by Ghosh (1996) and Narayanamoorthy (2001) to study the incidence of poverty earlier.

As per Table 5.1, the average PFG was 965 kg/ha in 1973-74, but it had increased to 2334.21 kg/ha in 2011-12. Average of CI had increased from 122.61 per cent in 1973-74 to 142.65 per cent during 2011-12. Similarly, average of RWRAL, FPHRP and SDAPHRP were 9.36 (Rs.), 281.23 (kg.) and 892.86 (Rs.) respectively during 1973-74 but in 2011-12, RWRAL was 30.56 (Rs.), FPHRP, 455.01 (kg.) and SDAPHRP, 1500.41 (Rs.). In the case of the main variable called IAPTRP, average was 90.33 during 1973-74, which increased to 160.75 during 2011-12. Likewise, the average of GIAGCA was 26.87 per cent in 1973-74, but it has increased to 51.49 per cent in 2011-12. However, the value of dependent variable PRP decreased from 53.86 per cent in 1973-74 to 11.48 per cent in 2011-12. This implies that while the above poverty determinant variables had increased from 1973-74 to 2011-12, PRP had decreased during the same period (see, Table 5.2). It is understood that these poverty determinant variables were responsible for reducing rural poverty. As explained in the methodology chapter, both descriptive and regression analysis were carried out to analyse the impact of irrigation on rural poverty across State-level in India.

5.3. Incidence of Poverty and Characteristics of the States

In this section, an attempt has been made to classify the States into Above National Average (ANA) and Below the National Average (BNA) in terms of percentage of population below the poverty line and study their irrigation-related characteristics at all eight time points: 1973-74, 1977-78, 1983, 1987-88, 1993-94, 1999-2000, 2004-05 and

Table 5.2: Data on Rural Poverty and Ranks of each State, 1973-74 to 2011-12

States	*Rural Poverty (%)*							
	1973-74	*1977-78*	*1983*	*1987-88*	*1993-94*	*1999-2000*	*2004-05*	*2011-12*
Andhra Pradesh	48.41 (10)	38.11 (11)	26.53 (12)	20.92 (12)	15.92 (13)	11.05 (11)	11.20 (13)	10.96 (12)
Bihar	62.99 (3)	63.25 (4)	64.37 (2)	52.63 (2)	58.21 (1)	44.30 (2)	42.10 (2)	34.06 (3)
Gujarat	46.35 (11)	41.76 (10)	29.80 (11)	28.67 (11)	22.18 (12)	13.17 (10)	19.10 (9)	21.54 (8)
Haryana	34.23 (13)	27.73 (12)	20.56 (13)	16.22 (13)	28.02 (9)	8.27 (13)	13.60 (11)	11.64 (11)
Karnataka	55.14 (9)	48.18 (8)	36.33 (9)	32.82 (9)	29.88 (8)	17.38 (8)	20.80 (8)	24.53 (5)
Kerala	59.19 (5)	51.48 (7)	39.03 (8)	29.10 (10)	25.76 (11)	9.38 (12)	13.20 (12)	9.14 (13)
Madhya Pradesh	62.66 (4)	62.52 (5)	48.90 (5)	41.92 (5)	40.64 (5)	37.06 (3)	36.90 (3)	35.74 (1)
Maharashtra	57.71 (6)	63.97 (3)	45.23 (7)	40.78 (7)	37.93 (6)	23.72 (6)	29.60 (5)	24.22 (6)
Odisha	67.28 (2)	72.38 (1)	67.53 (1)	57.64 (1)	49.72 (2)	48.01 (1)	46.80 (1)	35.65 (2)
Punjab	28.21 (14)	16.37 (14)	13.20 (14)	12.60 (14)	11.95 (14)	6.35 (14)	9.10 (14)	7.66 (14)
Rajasthan	44.76 (12)	35.89 (13)	33.50 (10)	33.21 (8)	26.46 (10)	13.74 (9)	18.70 (10)	16.05 (9)
Tamil Nadu	57.43 (7)	57.68 (6)	53.99 (4)	45.80 (4)	32.48 (7)	20.55 (7)	22.80 (7)	15.83 (10)
Uttar Pradesh	56.53 (8)	47.60 (9)	46.45 (6)	41.10 (6)	42.28 (3)	31.22 (5)	33.40 (4)	30.40 (4)
West Bengal	73.16 (1)	68.34 (2)	63.05 (3)	48.30 (3)	40.80 (4)	31.85 (4)	28.60 (6)	22.52 (7)
All-India	56.44	53.07	45.65	39.09	37.27	27.09	28.30	25.70

Note: Figures in brackets are 'Ranks'.

Sources: Planning Commission (2014).

2011-12. As the level of poverty is determined by many factors and their complex interactions, States were divided into two groups: one with percentage of rural poverty above the national average and the other with percentage of rural poverty below the national average, for all eight time points, to understand the unique characteristics of these groups. Here also it is proposed to show the importance of irrigation in determining the incidence of poverty. For analysing the characteristics of ANA and BNA States, all the variables (IAPTRP, RWAL, FGP, SDAPHRP, CI and FPHRP), which were discussed in the earlier section were considered.

States that come under ANA group and BNA group in terms of percentage of poverty and their characteristics are presented in Table 5.3. The expectation of the analysis is that the BNA group of States will have significantly higher IAPTRP than the ANA group of States. As expected, IAPTRP was significantly higher for the group of BNA States when compared to the group of ANA States at all eight points of time considered for the analysis. While the average IAPTRP was 136.84 ha for the group of BNA States in 1973-74, it was only about 55.44 hectare for the group of ANA States. Similarly, for the year 1987-88, while the average of IAPTRP was 111.17 hectare for the group of BNA States, it was only 58.03 hectares for the States belonging to the group of ANA States, showing a significant difference. This trend has been observed in the recent years too. For instance, the average IAPTRP was 179.87 hectare for the BNA States and only 112.97 hectare for the group of ANA States for the year 2011-12.

The percentage of population living below poverty in rural areas had declined substantially at the national level (from 56.44% in 1973-74 to 25.70% in 2011-12) between the early 1970s and the end of the 2000s. However, the reduction is not the same across the States. While the rate of reduction was significant in States like Andhra Pradesh, Gujarat, Haryana, Karnataka, Madhya Pradesh, Kerala and West Bengal, it was less than the national level average in other States (see, Table 5.3). With regard to individual States, despite a significant reduction in the level of poverty between 1973-74 and 2011-12, States like Odisha, Bihar, Madhya Pradesh and Uttar Pradesh continued to record a higher percentage of population below the poverty line in 2011-12. In all these States, the level of IAPTRP was lower than the national-level average in the remaining States. The percentage of rural poverty was not only less in the States of Punjab, Haryana, Gujarat, Rajasthan and Tamil Nadu, but also declined significantly between 1973-74 and 2011-12, possibly because of higher IAPTRP. This suggests the important role played by IAPTRP in reducing poverty in rural areas.

This is found to be very much true for all other remaining time points taken for the analysis (see, Figure 5.1). As far as other characteristics of the ANA and BNA States were concerned, as shown

Table 5.3: States Having Above National Average (ANA) and Below National Average (BNA) in terms of Rural Poverty and Their Characteristics

Year	*States*	*IAPTRP*	*RWRAL*	*PFG*	*SDAPHRP*	*CI*	*FPHRP*
1973-74							
ANA	Bihar, Kerala, MP, MAH, Odisha, TN, UP, WB	55.44	8.20	940.00	703.69	123.26	207.99
BNA	AP, Gujarat, Haryana, Karnataka, Punjab, RAJ	136.84	10.90	998.33	1171.48	121.75	378.88
1977-78							
ANA	Bihar, MP, MAH, Odisha, TN, WB	52.74	8.25	1000.00	698.44	126.00	232.97
BNA	AP, Gujarat, Haryana, Karnataka, Kerala, Punjab, RAJ, UP	106.63	12.50	1207.50	831.18	126.56	325.56
1983							
ANA	Bihar, MP, Odisha, TN, UP, WB	70.95	9.14	1193.33	464.48	2558.80	263.41
BNA	AP, Gujarat, Haryana, Karnataka, Kerala, MAH, Punjab, RAJ	118.80	13.73	1376.25	613.01	128.11	426.05
1987-88							
ANA	Bihar, MP, MAH, Odisha, TN, UP, WB	58.03	11.77	1210.00	376.23	133.98	218.89
BNA	AP, Gujarat, Haryana, Karnataka, Kerala, Punjab, RAJ	111.17	17.37	1440.00	627.99	129.78	336.25
1993-94							
ANA	Bihar, MP, MAH, Odisha, UP, WB	70.86	14.28	1435.00	462.46	140.04	281.98
BNA	AP, Gujarat, Haryana, Karnataka, Kerala, Punjab, RAJ, TN	120.61	19.31	1858.75	704.52	134.20	435.99
1999-2000							
ANA	Bihar, MP, Odisha, UP, WB	67.48	16.14	1639.20	1206.27	146.08	253.69
BNA	AP, Gujarat, Haryana, Karnataka, Kerala, MAH, Punjab, RAJ, TN	105.60	23.25	1974.67	2346.76	134.90	428.58
2004-05							
ANA	Bihar, MP, MAH, Odisha, UP, WB	66.45	17.33	1480.38	1295.67	146.28	212.24

(Contd.)

Year	*States*	*IAPTRP*	*RWRAL*	*PFG*	*SDAPHRP*	*CI*	*FPHRP*
BNA	AP, Gujarat, Haryana, Karnataka, Kerala, Punjab, RAJ, TN	117.10	27.94	2152.65	2358.34	138.94	457.66
2011-12							
ANA	Bihar, MP, Odisha, UP	112.97	22.42	1852.25	956.53	139.63	301.47
BNA	AP, Gujarat, Haryana, Karnataka, Kerala, MAH, Punjab, RAJ, TN, WB	179.87	33.82	2527.00	1717.96	143.86	516.43

Notes: AP: Andhra Pradesh; MP: Madhya Pradesh; MAH: Maharashtra; RAJ: Rajasthan; TN: Tamil Nadu; UP: Uttar Pradesh; WB: West Bengal.

Sources: Same as in Table 5.1.

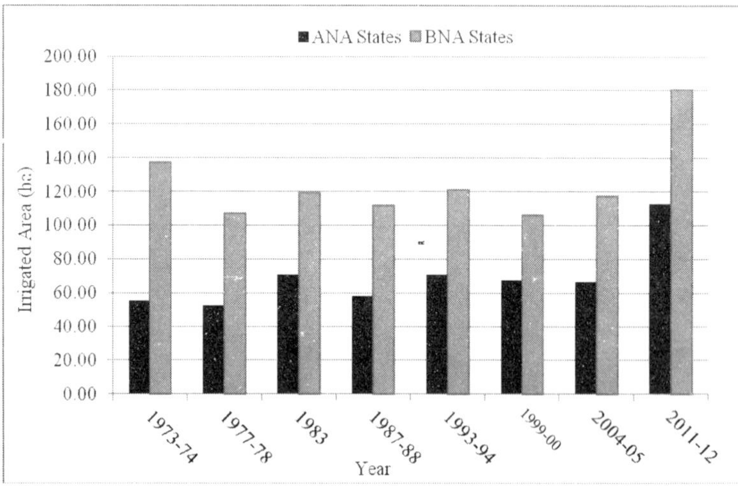

Fig. 5.1: Irrigated Area Per Thousand Rural Population for ANA and BNA Group of States in terms of Rural Poverty

in the earlier section, the average values of RWAL, SDAPHRP and FPHRP were much lower for the group of ANA States than for those of the BNA States group. All these suggest that irrigation played a significant catalytic role in increasing the real wage rate for the agricultural labourers, SDAPHRP and FPHRP. It needs to be mentioned here that all these variables were also considered as important determinants of poverty by the existing studies on rural poverty.

5.4. Irrigation and Poverty Nexus

As mentioned earlier, the study by Narayanamoorthy (2001) was probably the first study that directly related the irrigation factor with rural poverty by using simple regression analysis, but this study had covered only four time points, namely 1973-74, 1977-78, 1983, and 1987-88. Since, many unprecedented changes have taken place in agriculture and rural economy of India after 1987-88, this study tries to bring out the role of irrigation in determining the level of poverty in rural India, covering the data up to 2011-12, which is the latest data available on rural poverty by States in India when this chapter was completed. Moreover, these existing studies have not used irrigation as a lagged variable in their regression analysis, which is essential because irrigation facility cannot instantaneously impact on rural poverty. Keeping this in view, correlation values were computed, using both irrigation-related and non-irrigation-related variables and regressions were computed using only irrigation (IAPTRP) as the independent variable determining the incidence of rural poverty. First of all, results obtained out of the correlations presented in Table 5.4, have shown a significant negative relationship with the percentage of population below the poverty line at all eight time points, suggesting that the level of poverty was lower in States where RWAL, PFG, SDAPHRP, CI and FPHRP were higher. With regard to the irrigation-related variable, a very strong inverse relationship can be observed between IAPTRP and PRP at all eight time points. This clearly shows that irrigation is an important factor associated with the level of poverty in rural India.

Table 5.4: Correlation Value: Percentage of Rural Poverty with Other Associated Variables

Variable	*1973-74*	*1977-78*	*1983*	*1987-88*	*1993-94*	*1999-2000*	*2004-05*	*2011-12*
GIAGCA	–0.62[a]	–0.65[a]	–0.51[c]	–0.52[b]	–0.30[ns]	–0.24[ns]	–0.20[ns]	–0.25[ns]
IAPTRP	–0.87[a]	–0.82[a]	–0.69[a]	–0.66[a]	–0.49[c]	–0.51[c]	–0.48[c]	–0.44[d]
RWAL	–0.65[a]	–0.73[a]	–0.71[a]	–0.59[b]	–0.49[c]	–0.61[a]	–0.49[c]	–0.79[a]
PFG	–0.32[ns]	–0.46[c]	–0.49[c]	–0.48[c]	–0.38[d]	–0.45[c]	–0.59[b]	–0.65[a]
SDAPHRP	–0.82[a]	–0.47[c]	–0.44[d]	–0.65[a]	–0.60[b]	–0.65[a]	–0.71[a]	–0.52[c]
CI	–0.37[d]	–0.23[ns]	–0.36[ns]	–0.054[ns]	–0.01[ns]	–0.04[ns]	–0.09[ns]	–0.26[ns]
FPHRP	–0.74[a]	–0.67[a]	–0.63[a]	–0.54[b]	–0.42[d]	–0.39[d]	–0.46[c]	–0.45[d]

Notes: a, b, c and d are significant level at 1, 5, 10 and 20 per cent respectively; ns—not significant.

Sources: Same as in Table 5.1.

The purpose of the study was not only to quantify the impact of irrigation on the rural poverty, but also to examine whether the poverty-reducing impact of irrigation had increased or decreased over the years. In order to understand this relationship, three different regression models were organised by using ordinary least squares method involving IAPTRP as an explanatory variable, with a time lag of 5 years, with time lag of 10 years and also without any time lag for all eight time points. In fact, factors like RWAL, SDAPHRP, FPHRP etc., have significant influence on the level of poverty. However, the study excluded these variables while computing the regression equation mainly because of three reasons. First, the main aim of the study was to demonstrate the impact of irrigation on rural poverty and not to explain total variation in poverty across States. Second, as mentioned earlier, these variables are not the major independent variables because the level of irrigation highly influenced these variables. Third, there is a possibility of multi-collinearity when these variables are included along with IAPTRP and high correlation among these variables was reported. Due to these reasons, regression was arranged using only irrigation (IAPTRP) as a single explanatory variable to relate to the level of poverty in rural India. The results of regression results estimated without giving any time lag for IAPTRP variable are presented in Table 5.5.

The regression results show that there was significant inverse relationship between the level of rural poverty and the density of irrigated area, standardised by rural population (irrigated area per thousand rural populations). Though the results undoubtedly confirm that the development of irrigation reduced rural poverty, the strength of the regression coefficients, along with R^2, declined consistently from 1973-74 to 2011-12. For instance, while one hectare increase in IAPTRP reduced rural poverty by about 0.15 per cent in 1973-74 and 0.13 per cent in 1987-88, the extent of reduction was only 0.03 per cent in 2011-12, when all 14 States were considered for the regression analysis. These results confirm our theoretical hypothesis of irrigation having a positive impact on rural poverty. However, such impact cannot be unidirectional in the sense that reduction in the pace of irrigation may not increase poverty or reduce the pace of poverty reduction. The reasons are obvious and this can be explained with the help of growth in an agricultural dependent population, relationship between agricultural and non-agricultural income and elasticity of such a relationship as well as growth in real wages.

Table 5.5: Impact of Irrigation (IAPTRP) on Rural Poverty: Linear Regression Results

Year	Dependent Variable	Model (1): $PRP_t = F(IAPTRP_t)$			
		Constant	Slope	R^2	N
1973-74	PRP	67.58[a] (2.73)	–0.152[a] (0.03)	0.77	14
1977-78	PRP	67.32[a] (4.28)	–0.21[a] (0.04)	0.69	14
1983	PRP	57.26[a] (5.64)	–0.15[a] (0.04)	0.49	14
1987-88	PRP	46.95[a] (4.56)	–0.13[a] (0.04)	0.45	14
1993-94	PRP	42.07[a] (5.52)	–0.09[c] (0.05)	0.25	14
1999-2000	PRP	33.61[a] (6.43)	–0.12[c] (0.06)	0.26	14
2004-05	PRP	33.41[a] (5.34)	–0.09[c] (0.05)	0.24	14
2011-12	PRP	26.93[a] (4.04)	–0.03[c] (0.02)	0.19	14
Pooled (1973-2012)	PRP	47.01 (2.32)	–0.12[a] (.02)	0.27	112

Notes: Figures in the brackets are 't' value; [a] and [c] are significant level at 1 and 10 per cent respectively; t is time lag.

Sources: Same as in Table 5.1.

Development of irrigation cannot make a significant impact instantaneously on rural poverty in any given region. Irrigation benefit flows on certain pathways to finally make an impact on the poor person, which normally takes time. Irrigation availability initially changes the land-use pattern, including its intensity, increases the adoption of technological inputs and then brings about changes in cropping patterns from low-value to high-value crops, improves the cropping intensity and then increases the production and productivity of crops. These changes increase not only the demand for labour but also the wage rate for agricultural labourers, among whom the incidence of poverty is very high in rural areas. The increased production of foodgrain owing to irrigation development also helps the rural poor to afford food at a cheaper rate, which ultimately helps them to cross poverty barriers. This entire process cannot take place instantaneously after the introduction of irrigation in any region. Therefore, it is necessary to use irrigation as a lagged variable in the regression analysis to capture its real impact on rural poverty.

Keeping this in view, regressions were estimated separately, treating irrigation with 5-year time lag ($PRP_t = \alpha + b_1 IAPTRP_{t-5}$) and also with 10 year time lag ($PRP_t = \alpha + b_1 IAPTRP_{t-10}$). The results show that the strength of impact of irrigation on reducing the rural poverty was much better compared to the regression results computed without any time lag (*see*, Tables 5.6 and 5.7). However, the strength of regression coefficients and the R^2 was declining over time even when irrigation was used as a lagged variable in the regression analysis. Does this mean that the irrigation is not very important in reducing rural poverty today in India? One cannot completely discard the relevance of irrigation in reducing rural poverty because even today when irrigation availability is reduced due to monsoon failures or other reasons, the production of foodgrain and other agricultural commodities declines sharply, which results in increased food inflation causing deep distress especially for the rural poor.

Table 5.6: Impact of Irrigation (IAPTRP) on Rural Poverty—Linear Regression Results Estimated Treating Irrigation with 5 Years Time Lag

Year	*Dependent Variable*	*Model (2): PRP = F ($IAPTRP_{t-5}$)*			
		Constant	*Slope*	*R^2*	*N*
1973-74	PRP	67.48[a] (3.04)	–0.17[a] (0.03)	0.73	14
1977-78	PRP	67.13[a] (3.99)	–0.19[a] (0.04)	0.72	14
1983	PRP	57.21[a] (5.58)	–0.18[a] (0.05)	0.48	14
1987-88	PRP	47.21[a] (4.70)	–0.12[a] (0.04)	0.45	14
1993-94	PRP	40.72[a] (5.06)	–0.09[c] (0.05)	0.24	14
1999-2000	PRP	31.23[a] (6.14)	–0.08[d] (0.05)	0.19	14
2004-05	PRP	33.96[a] (5.57)	–0.10[c] (0.05)	0.24	14
2011-12	PRP	27.78[a] (4.63)	–0.07[c] (0.04)	0.18	14

Notes: Figures in the brackets are 't' value; [a, c] and [d] are significant level at 1, 10 and 20 per cent respectively; t–5 is time lag.

Sources: Same as in Table 5.1.

The reduced strength of regression coefficients of irrigation over time can be attributed to a few important factors. First, unlike in the

1960s, 1970s and 1980s, the rural non-agricultural income (earnings) has been growing faster than agricultural income, especially for agricultural labourers during the last two decades, as confirmed by various studies (Vaidyanathan, 1994; Visaria and Basant, 1994; Nayyar, 1996; Binswanger-Mkhize, 2013; Jatav and Sen, 2013). This possibly could have weakened the relationship between irrigation and rural poverty. Second, looking from another angle, the relationship might have weakened due to the intensity of various anti-poverty programmes implemented in the late 1970s, increased in its spread, in the mid-1980s and in the 2000s. A quality change in the anti-poverty programmes towards employment generation such as MGNREGS also could have made the difference. On the whole, one can say from the above analysis that the decline of a relationship between rural poverty and irrigation was possibly more due to significant increase of rural non-agricultural income than due to agricultural income during the last two decades.

Table 5.7: Impact of Irrigation (IAPTRP) on Rural Poverty—Linear Regression Results Estimated Treating Irrigation with 10 Years Time Lag

Year	*Dependent Variable*	*Model (3): PRP = F ($IAPTRP_{t-10}$)*			
		Constant	*Slope*	*R^2*	*N*
1977-78	PRP	67.14[a] (4.28)	–0.22[a] (0.04)	0.68	14
1983	PRP	57.09[a] (5.34)	–0.17[a] (0.05)	0.51	14
1987-88	PRP	47.75[a] (4.64)	–0.14[a] (0.04)	0.46	14
1993-94	PRP	41.97[a] (5.09)	–0.09[b] (0.04)	0.28	14
1999-2000	PRP	30.31[a] (5.55)	–0.09[c] (0.05)	0.21	14
2004-05	PRP	31.97[a] (5.31)	–0.07[d] (0.04)	0.18	14
2011-12	PRP	28.17[a] (4.83)	–0.07[c] (0.05)	0.18	14

Notes: Figures in the brackets are 't' value; [a, b, c] and [d] are significant level at 1, 5, 10 and per cent respectively; t–10 is time lag.

Sources: Same as in Table 5.1.

5.5. Conclusion

Although irrigation plays an important role in reducing the rural poverty, the researchers have not explicitly brought out this relationship. An attempt has been made in this study to understand the role of irrigation in the reduction of the level of rural poverty in India by taking cross-section data of 14 major States at eight points of time: 1973-74, 1977-78, 1983, 1987-88, 1993-94, 1999-2000, 2004-05 and 2011-12. While analysing the importance of irrigation empirically, the study shows through regression analyses that there was clear significant inverse relationship between the incidence of rural poverty and the irrigated area per thousand rural people at all eight time points considered for the analysis. The study also finds that the strength of inverse relationship between irrigation availability and the rural poverty was better when irrigation was used as lagged variable, meaning that the base-level irrigation was also important in reducing the rural poverty.

6

Irrigation and Rural Poverty Nexus

A District Level Analysis

6.1. Introduction

It is known historically that the central factor of poverty reduction is economic growth (Dollar and Kraay, 2000; Fan *et al.*, 1999; Thirtle *et al.*, 2001). The rising poverty in most cases was the result of poor governance and slow economic growth (Asian Development Bank, 2002). Agricultural growth plays a major role for sustained and stable economic growth especially in developing countries like India. Agriculture supplies food to the people, raw materials to the industries, exports to the traders, employment to the farm and non-farm sector, releases surplus capital and it stimulates demand for local goods and services (Wiggins, 2001). Agricultural growth can thus strengthen economic growth and when it is labour intensive, it can be highly poverty reducing because it is geographically distributed (Lipton, 1977). Since the levels of poverty were somewhat higher in the rural areas relative to those in urban settings, agriculture is the central driver for alleviating poverty in rural area (Asian Development Bank, 2002).

There are some studies which indicate inverse relationship between agricultural growth and the incidence of rural poverty (Ahluwalia, 1978; Sundaram and Tendulkar, 1988; Ghosh, 1996; Ravallion and Datt, 1996; Datt and Revallion, 1996; Bhattarai and Narayanamoorthy, 2003; Hussain *et al.*, 2007; Thorat and Fan, 2007; Janvry and Sadoulet, 2010). In fact, there is positive impact of agricultural growth on rural poverty and irrigation is the main factor that determines the growth of agriculture. There are studies on the importance of irrigation and agricultural growth in India (Dhawan,

1988; Rath and Mitra, 1989; Vaidyanathan *et al.*, 1994; Narayanamoorthy, 2001; Bhattarai and Narayanamoorthy, 2003; Narayanamoorthy, 2007). Irrigation contributes to agricultural growth by raising the productivity of land and !abour (Smith, 2004; Vaidyanathan *et al.*, 1994). The positive impact of irrigation on intensification of agriculture and on increased crop productivity and farm income has been well documented by various studies in the context of Asian agriculture (Mellor, 1985, 1996, 2002; Dhawan, 1988; Lipton and Litchfield, 2002; Bhattarai and Narayanamoorthy, 2003; Narayanamoorthy and Deshpande, 2003; Narayanamoorthy and Hanjra, 2006; Narayanamoorthy, 2001, 2007). Irrigation is believed to have benefited the population by providing more food at reduced prices (Hussain and Hanjra, 2004; Hussain *et al.*, 2006). Due to irrigation, the farm productivity increases and this surplus production lowers food prices. Thus, the real income of the consumers increases because of the price fall for food. This reduces poverty because the purchasing power of the majority of poor households in rural areas increases and then they spend a high proportion of their income on consumer products.

Irrigation resources have played a major role historically in poverty alleviation by ensuring agricultural development, expanding livelihood opportunities, increasing the use of yield increasing inputs, cropping intensity and productivity of the crops, providing additional employment opportunities, both on and off the farm and pushing up the wage rates for agricultural labourers (Dhawan, 1991; Ray, 1992; Vaidyanathan, 1994a, 1994b; Reddy, 1995; Narayanamoorthy, 2001; Hussain and Hanjra, 2004; Hussain *et al.*, 2006; Ghosh *et al.*, 2011, 2012). Thus, empirical evidence suggests that irrigation has reduced rural poverty (Narayanamoorthy, 2001; Bhattarai and Narayanamoorthy, 2003; Hussain and Hanjra, 2004; Shah and Singh, 2004; Smith, 2004; Lipton, 2007; and Hussain, 2007; Narayanamoorthy, 2007). If irrigation has such vitality, why are such impacts not being replicated at district-level study in India? The missing links between irrigation and rural poverty have been focused in this chapter. There are studies available on the impact of irrigation on rural poverty by using State-level data across India. However, there are only limited studies on relationship between irrigation and poverty, using district-level data across India. In this chapter, therefore, an attempt has been made to study the irrigation and rural poverty nexus across districts in India. The specific objectives of this chapter are: (1) to analyse the impact of irrigation on rural poverty across the districts in India; and (2) to study the relationship between base level irrigation and rural poverty.

Table 6.1: Number of Districts Selected from 13 Different States

States	*No. of Districts*	*Rural Poverty*	
		Average (%)	*SD*
Andhra Pradesh	15	9.80	7.99
Bihar	6	41.35	16.87
Gujarat	10	29.06	22.79
Haryana	6	8.50	5.09
Karnataka	13	26.71	15.65
Madhya Pradesh	28	43.00	14.97
Maharashtra	16	38.96	10.71
Odisha	9	48.70	19.92
Punjab	11	7.17	7.22
Rajasthan	19	21.15	11.15
Tamil Nadu	6	16.95	5.89
Uttar Pradesh	28	26.00	9.44
West Bengal	11	31.15	13.12
Total	**178**	**28.10**	**17.65**

Note: SD—Standard Deviation.

Source: Chaudhuri and Gupta (2009).

The study was carried out entirely based on secondary data, pertaining to four time points, namely 1970-71, 1980-81, 1990-91 and 2000-01. For the purpose of the analysis, a total of 178 districts were selected from 13 States of India. As mentioned in the methodology chapter, data were collected and computed from various sources. Like the State-level analysis, both descriptive and regressions analysis were used to study the relationship between irrigation and rural poverty at the district-level. These 178 districts recorded an average 28.10 per cent of rural poverty with the standard deviation of 17.65 (*see*, Table 6.1).

6.2. Description of Variables Used in the Study for Analysis

As mentioned earlier, poverty is determined by various factors. However, this study relied only on seven important poverty determinant variables (CI, ELE, GCAPTRP, GIAGCA, LITE, ROAD and WAGE) due to non-availability of data for the selected period of time (*see*, Table 6.2). It was assumed that these variables would greatly influence the rural poverty (PRP) across space and time. The study considered the variable PRP as the dependent variable in the analysis, which is expressed in terms of Percentage of Rural Poverty (PRP). It is very well documented that there exists an inverse correlation between irrigation development and rural poverty (Narayanamoorthy, 2001; Bhattarai and Narayanamoorthy, 2003; Hussain and Hanjra, 2004; Smith, 2004; Lipton, 2007; and Hussain, 2007; Narayanamoorthy, 2007; Ghosh, 2001, 2012). In order to represent the irrigation in the analysis, the percentage of Gross Irrigated Area to Gross Cropped Area (GIAGCA) was used. Cropping Intensity (CI), defined as the ratio of gross cropped area to net cropped area in percentage term, explains how intensively crops are cultivated in a year. Since agriculture directly impacts on rural poverty and agriculture is determined by the intensive of crop cultivation, CI was included for the analysis along with other variables (Narayanamoorthy and Hanjra, 2006).

Another important indicator that would positively and directly contribute to the agriculture development and indirectly influence the rural poverty is the total number of villages electrified (ELE). The rural electrification is bound to have a direct impact on the use of motor pump sets for irrigation purpose, which will increase the agricultural production and productivity and then reduce rural poverty. The road variable (ROAD) which is represented by the percentage of villages having road facility is indeed an indicator of the development of transport infrastructure and undisputedly is the most important element in alleviating rural poverty. Though there is still no consensus on exactly how roads become critical to agriculture development, yet majority of studies point out that those using with better roads can drastically reduce the cost of inputs and can increase the scope of profitable trade. GCAPTRP is indicated by the coverage of gross cropped area per thousand rural population which represents density of population in the cropped area. It is well documented that if GCAPTRP increases, then cropped area is more and population is less, which implies more production and less population. RWRAL has been considered as one of the important variables for studying the incidence of rural poverty by some earlier studies (Ghosh, 1996). State-level analysis shows that RWRAL is positively influenced by the development of irrigation (Parthasarathy, 1996; Narayanamoorthy, 2001). The development of irrigation increases the intensity of cultivation, which in turn increases the demand for farm labourers. This process helps to increase the money wage rates and employment days for agricultural labourers and in the process, total earning increases. Thus, increased income of agricultural labourers increases the living standard of rural population.

To study the influence of poverty determinant variables on rural poverty, a brief discussion is necessary to explain what the poverty determinant variables at the district-level stand for. To begin with, it is observed from Table 6.2 that on an average, about 119.69 per cent of cropping intensity, in each of the selected districts during 1970-71, had increased to 141.55 per cent in 2000-01. The increased cropping intensity implies that the land intensity for cultivation had increased from 1970-71 to 2000-01. Wage rate increased from Rs. 4.29 to Rs. 76.47 for the same period. However, density of population to cropped area decreased from 487.31 hectare to 406.08 hectare from 1970-71 to 2000-01. While the GIAGCA increased from 24.50 per cent to 43.69 per cent in 2000-01, villages having *pucca* road facility increased from 29.42 per cent to around 61.86 per cent during the same period.

Table 6.2: Description of Variables used in District Level Study for Analysis

Variables	*Description*	*Unit*	*Average*			
			1970-71	1980-81	1990-91	2000-01
CI	Cropping intensity	%	119.69 (19.62)	127.33 (19.88)	133.90 (23.78)	141.55 (29.15)
ELEC	Percentage of village electrified	%	24.06 (24.56)	53.68 (28.27	80.07 (21.75)	87.71 (16.71)
GCAPTRP	Gross cropped area per thousand rural population	ha	487.31 (275.40)	468.26 (270.28)	435.70 (280.59)	406.08 (552.09)
GIAGCA	Percentage of irrigated area to gross cropped area	%	24.50 (21.87)	31.10 (24.09)	38.49 (25.84)	43.69 (25.38)
LITE	Percentage of rural literacy rate	%	21.13 (8.27)	27.55 (12.65)	41.78 (12.89)	56.36 (14.18)
ROAD	Percentage of villages having road facility	%	29.42 (13.75)	39.92 (24.08)	47.27 (24.85)	61.86 ((23.59)
WAGE	Average wages of skilled and unskilled rural male labourers	Rs./day	4.29 (1.80)	9.78 (3.98)	31.26 (11.27)	76.47 (29.64)

Note: Figures in the brackets are Standard Deviation.

Sources: Census of India (various years); GoI (various years); Bhalla and Singh (2010, 2012).

Similarly, the rural literacy rate (LITE) increased from 21.13 per cent to 56.36 per cent and coverage of rural electrification (ELEC) increased from 24.06 per cent to 87.71 per cent during the same period. This increased electricity, literacy rate and wage rate and road connectivity had positive impact on rural poverty. But, due to increased population, the density of cropped was reduced during the decades in each of the selected districts. All these clearly suggest that the poverty determinants variable had expanded considerably during 1970-71 to 2000-01. It is clear that there was appreciable improvement in the poverty determinant variables such as irrigation, cropping intensity, density of population with regard to cropped area, supply of electricity to villages, road facilities, literacy rate and wage rate of male across the districts during 1970-71 and 2000-01. The information on irrigation was very vital in this analysis as it would help analysing the behaviour of rural poverty of the selected districts. If the selected districts recorded an average of irrigation above or below the average of 178 districts, what does it tell and more importantly, how significant is it with respect to rural poverty? All these questions can be answered only by analysing the data of selected districts which are discussed in the following sections.

6.3. Incidence of Poverty and Characteristics of Districts

A major objective of this chapter is to find out whether the irrigation has any relationship with the rural poverty, across the districts in India. Generally, irrigation increases agricultural production and productivity, increases cropping intensity, enhances employment and income and helps to increase the purchasing power of poor. Expanded production lowers food price and makes food affordable to the rural people. In order to study this, the present study categorised the districts into two: as districts with Above the Average (AA) districts (178 districts) and districts with Below the Average (BA) districts (178 districts) for all the four points of time; 1970-71, 1980-81, 1990-91 and 2000-01. How the AA and BA districts rank in terms of poverty determinant parameters over time is evident from the data presented in Table 6.3?

As regards the characteristics of the districts, a distinct difference in all the parameters between the AA and BA districts across all three time points is evident. Among the poverty determinant variables, namely CI, ELEC, GCAPTRP, GIAGCA,

LITE, ROAD and WAGE, the difference between AA and BA districts is more pronounced in GIAGCA for all the four time points. While the GIAGCA of AA districts was 10.86 per cent and districts with BA were 34.66 per cent in 1970-71, the same was 34.30 per cent in AA districts and 50.69 per cent in BA districts in 2000-01. This suggests that districts having higher irrigation coverage recorded lower poverty rate.

Table 6.3: Characteristics of the Districts Classified Based on Percentage of Rural Population Below Poverty Line (2004-05)

Classification	*No. of Districts*	*CI (%)*	*ELEC (%)*	*GCAPTRP (ha)*	*GIAGCA (%)*	*LITE (%)*	*ROAD (%)*	*WAGE (Rs./day)*
1970-71								
AA Districts	76	116.01 (18.22)	12.84 (13.65)	522.91 (306.30)	10.86 (10.00)	19.23 (6.79)	23.23 (8.00)	3.58 (0.88)
BA Districts	102	122.43 (20.25)	32.43 (27.44)	460.77 (248.17)	34.66 (22.80)	22.55 (9.00)	34.02 (15.29)	4.81 (2.12)
All Average	178	119.69 (19.62)	24.06 (24.56)	487.31 (275.40)	24.50 (21.87)	21.13 (8.27)	29.42 (13.75)	4.29 (1.80)
1980-81								
AA Districts	76	121.89 (16.26)	38.73 (21.74)	487.87 (271.63)	16.48 (13.98)	24.82 (8.48)	26.29 (11.20)	8.21 (1.87)
BA Districts	102	131.39 (21.38)	64.83 (27.49)	453.64 (269.68)	42.00 (24.32)	29.59 (14.74)	50.09 (26.05)	10.95 (4.68)
Ali Average	178	127.33 (19.88)	53.68 (28.27)	468.26 (270.28)	31.10 (24.09)	27.55 (12.65)	39.92 (24.08)	9.78 (3.98)
1990-91								
AA Districts	76	129.75 (20.70)	74.03 (22.35)	449.98 (245.59)	24.89 (17.59)	39.43 (11.39)	33.18 (14.79)	27.30 (6.06)
BA Districts	102	136.99 (25.50)	84.58 (20.25)	425.05 (304.83)	48.62 (26.40)	43.53 (13.70)	57.77 (25.67)	34.21 (13.21)
All Average	178	133.90 (23.78)	80.07 (21.75)	435.70 (280.59)	38.49 (25.84)	41.78 (12.89)	47.27 (24.85)	31.26 (11.27)
2000-01								
AA Districts	76	135.80 (24.60)	83.57 (18.55)	503.34 (783.16)	34.30 (21.87)	56.94 (13.21)	49.36 (20.93)	64.34 (19.88)
BA Districts	102	145.84 (31.56)	90.79 (14.55)	333.61 (257.46)	50.69 (25.66)	55.93 (14.92)	71.18 (21.08)	85.52 (32.44)
All Average	178	141.55 (29.15)	87.71 (16.71)	406.08 (552.09)	43.69 (25.36)	56.36 (14.18)	61.86 (23.59)	76.47 (29.64)

Note: Figures in the brackets are standard deviation.
Sources: Same as in Tables 6.2.

After studying the characteristics of the districts based on rural poverty the following classification was done by dividing 178 districts into three categories, namely Districts with Severe Poverty (DSP), Districts with Medium Poverty (DMP) and Districts with Lower Poverty (DLP), to understand the nexus between irrigation and rural poverty. The analysis reveals that the rural poverty was severe in districts where GIAGCA was low as compared to districts with medium poverty for all four point-times. Those districts with lower poverty recorded better GIAGCA than districts with medium poverty during the same period of time (see, Table 6.4). Irrigation was relatively higher among the districts whose average GIAGCA was below the average GIAGCA of 178 districts than in the case of districts whose GIAGCA was above the average GIAGCA (see, Table 6.4). It shows the irrigation impact on rural poverty reduction vividly.

Table 6.4: Classification of Districts Based on Poverty and their GIAGCA and IAPTRP

Classification	*No. of Districts*	*GIAGCA (%)*				*IAPTRP (ha)*			
		2000-01	1990-91	1980-81	1970-71	2000-01	1990-91	1980-81	1970-71
Districts with Sever Poverty ($\bar{X}$ + SD)	34	8.01	12.30	18.83	27.52	34.32	52.65	76.04	115.20
Districts with Medium Poverty ($\bar{X}$ + SD) to ($\bar{X}$ – SD)	114	22.56	29.63	37.48	46.32	91.33	129.12	152.27	181.64
Districts with Lower Poverty ($\bar{X}$ – SD)	30	50.55	58.00	64.58	52.04	232.18	287.48	312.67	190.79

Sources: Computed using Bhalla and Singh (2010, 2012), Census of India (various years) and Chaudhuri and Gupta (2009).

In addition to studying the relationship between the GIAGCA and the rural poverty, an attempt has also been made to find out whether the Irrigation Area Per Thousand Rural Population (IAPTRP) had any association with the rural poverty during the period of analysis in all the 178 districts. It is clear from Table 6.4 that the districts with lower poverty recorded more IAPTRP than the districts with medium poverty and severe poverty for the four time points. However, this descriptive analysis is insufficient to decide clearly whether irrigation variables had better role than other factors. Therefore, the relationship between poverty and its determinant variables was investigated by using simple and multiple regression analysis.

6.4. Irrigation and Poverty Nexus

It is evident from the previous chapter on State-level analysis that development of irrigation cannot make a significant impact instantaneously on rural poverty in any given region. Irrigation benefit flows on certain pathways to finally make an impact on the poor people, which normally take time. Irrigation availability initially changes the land-use pattern (including its intensity), increases the adoption of technological inputs and then brings about changes in cropping patterns from low-value to high-value crops, improves the cropping intensity and then increases the production and productivity of crops. These changes increase not only the demand for labour but also the wage rate for agricultural labourers, among whom the incidence of poverty is very high in rural areas. The increased production of foodgrain owing to irrigation development also helps the rural poor to afford food at a cheaper rate, which ultimately helps them to cross poverty barriers. This entire process cannot take place instantaneously after the introduction of irrigation in any region. Therefore, it was necessary to use irrigation as a lagged variable in the regression analysis to capture its real impact on rural poverty. Keeping this in view, separate regressions were estimated, treating irrigation (GIAGCA) without time lag ($PRP_t = \alpha + b_1 GIAGCA$), with 10-year time lag ($PRP_t = \alpha + b_1 GIAGCA_{t-10}$), with 20-year time lag ($PRP_t = \alpha + b_1 GIAGCA_{t-20}$) and also with 30-year time lag ($PRP_t = \alpha + b_1 GIAGCA_{t-30}$). The results of the regression showed that the strength of impact of irrigation on reducing rural poverty was much stronger when irrigation was used as lagged variable as compared to the regression results computed by treating irrigation without any time lag (*see*, Table 5.5). In addition, the strength of regression coefficients and the R^2 also increased over time when irrigation was used as a lagged variable in the regression analysis for study period. The impact of irrigation on rural poverty is also clearly visible in the Fig. 6.1 because when trend of PRP is sloping downward, irrigation (GIAGCA) is increasing in a fluctuating manner over the period.

Table 6.5: Impact of Irrigation (GIAGCA) on Rural Poverty: Linear Regression Results

Model	*Results arrived using the data of 178 Districts*				
	Constant	*Slope*	R^2	*Adjusted* R^2	*N*
Model No. 4	39.570[a]	−0.262[a]	0.143	0.138	178
($PRP_t = \alpha + b_1\ GIAGCA_t$)	(16.151)	(−5.409)			
Model No. 5	42.75[a]	−0.381[a]	0.310	0.307	178
($PRP = \alpha + b_1\ GIAGCA_{t-10}$)	(21.592)	(−8.902)			
Model No. 6	41.740[a]	−0.438[a]	0.358	0.355	178
($PRP = \alpha + b_1\ GIAGCA_{t-20}$)	(24.015)	(--9.914)			
Model No. 7	40.090[a]	−0.489[a]	0.368	0.364	178
($PRP = \alpha + b_1\ GIAGCA_{t-30}$)	(25.283)	(−10.122)			

Note: Figures in the brackets are 't' value; t, t–10, t–20 and t–30 are time lag; a is significant level at 1 per cent.

Sources: Bhalla and Singh (2010, 2012) and Chaudhuri and Gupta (2009).

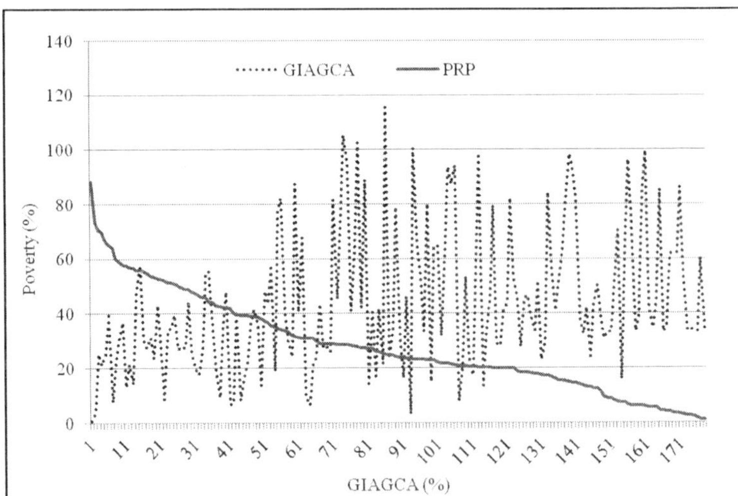

Fig. 6.1: District-wise Poverty Irrigation Nexus

Sources: Bhalla and Singh (2010, 2012) and Chaudhuri and Gupta (2009).

As was pointed out earlier, each of the variables that were taken up for the study would in one way or the other influence the rural poverty reduction. In order to find out the relationship between PRP and other poverty determinant variables, four types of multiple regressions were estimated keeping PRP as the dependent variable and other poverty determinant variables as independent variables. The four types of multiple regressions computed were: without time lag, with 10-year time lag, with 20-year time lag and with 30-year lag. From the regression results presented in Table 6.6, it is clear that all the variables included in the analysis under without time lag, determined rural poverty in one way or the other (in the year 2000-01). As expected, GIAGCA significantly influenced the rural poverty. The coefficient of irrigation (GIAGCA) turned out to be significantly negative, implying that GIAGCA determined the rural poverty. This means that GIAGCA and PRP were inversely associated and with an increase in irrigation, poverty decreased and *vice versa*. In addition, among all the variables selected for the regression analysis, irrigation seems to have played a major role in reducing rural poverty, when variables were used without time lag.

Table 6.6: Multivariate Regression Results: Factors Determine Rural Poverty in 178 Districts

Independent Variables	*Model No. (8) 2000-01*	*Model No. (9) 1990-91*	*Model No. (10) 1980-81*	*Model No. (11) 1970-71*
CI_t	0.016^{ns} (0.379)	0.068^{ns} (1.120)	0.147^{b} (2.000)	0.065^{ns} (1.073)
$ELEC_t$	-0.191^{a} (–2.492)	–0.037 $(-0.566)^{ns}$	-0.155^{b} (–2.347)	-0.076^{ns} (–0.046)
$GCAPTRP_t$	0.003^{d} (1.509)	0.001^{ns} (0.230)	0.007^{d} (1.510)	-0.002^{ns} (–0.580)
$GIAGCA_t$	-0.240^{a} (–5.135)	-0.309^{a} (–4.785)	-0.377^{a} (–5.128)	-0.416^{a} (–5.879)
$LITE_t$	0.145^{b} (1.780)	-0.028^{ns} (–0.299)	-0.011^{ns} (–0.114)	-0.123^{ns} (–0.814)
$ROAD_t$	-0.285^{a} (–5.561)	-0.220^{ns} (–3.049)	-0.030^{ns} (–0.351)	–0.087a (–0.698)
$WAGE_t$	-0.119^{a} (–3.093)	0.080^{ns} (0.573)	-0.292^{ns} (–0.829)	-0.400^{ns} (–0.516)
CONSTANT	70.454^{a} (8.674)	42.538^{a} (4.644)	30.680^{a} (3.324)	40.435^{a} (4.788)
R^2	0.445	0.405	0.454	0.405
Adjusted R^2	0.422	0.381	0.432	0.381
D-W	1.860	1.653	1.722	1.684
F	19.495	16.558	20.208	16.551
N	178	178	178	178

Notes: Figures in the brackets are 't' value; t, t–10, t–20 and t–30 are time lag; a, b and d are significant level at 1, 5 and 20 per cent respectively; ns–not significant.

Sources: Same as in Table 6.2.

Further, except the irrigation (GIAGCA), no other poverty determinant variable showed expected and significant results in all the models presented in Table 6.6. Irrigation increasingly and significantly influenced the rural poverty under without time lags to with time lag. The R^2 which was estimated to be 0.405 implies that about 40 per cent of the variations in rural poverty can be explained by the variables included in the regression analysis in 1970-71 (with 30 year time lag). Similarly, 45 per cent in 1980-81 (with 20 year time lag), 40 per cent in 1990-91 (with 10 year time lag) and 44 per cent (without any time lag) of the variation in rural poverty can be explained in 2000-01. It is found that the variation in explaining rural poverty decreased with time lag over the period. One percentage of increase in irrigation reduced 0.41 per cent of rural poverty in 1970-71 (with 30 year time lag). Likewise, irrigation reduced 0.37 per cent, 0.30 per cent and 0.24 per cent of rural poverty during 1980-81 (with 20 year time lag), 1990-91 (with 10 year time lag) and 2000-01 (without time lag) respectively.

The second most important variable in reducing rural poverty was wage rate. Due to increased wage rate, the income as well as consumption of rural people increased which finally reduced the rural poverty. On the whole, the regression analysis suggests that irrigation has consistently played a significant role in reducing rural poverty with and without time lag.

6.5. Conclusion

The main objective of this chapter was to analyse the impact of irrigation on rural poverty across districts of India. For this study, 178 districts from 13 States of India were considered. Both descriptive and regressions analysis were used, for the study. Simple and multiple regressions were used, by considering PRP as the dependent variable and other selected poverty determinant variables as independent variables, with time lag and without time lag for the analysis.

The descriptive analysis showed that the PRP was relatively high for those districts whose GIAGCA was below the average of 178 districts than those whose GIAGCA was higher than the average. The PRP was also found to be relatively high for those districts where IAPTRP was below the average of 178 districts. This means that there was an inverse relationship between irrigation and rural poverty. The simple and multiple regression analysis indicates that irrigation impact on alleviating rural poverty was better with time lag than without time lag.

7

Irrigation Impact on Rural Poverty

An Analysis of Survey Data

7.1. Introduction

A large number of studies have analysed the relationship between irrigation and agricultural growth, income of farmers etc. There are also studies available on the impact of irrigation on rural poverty using State-level data in India. However, there are no detailed studies available on source-wise irrigation and rural poverty nexus by using the field survey data. In this chapter, therefore, an attempt has been made to study the irrigation and rural poverty nexus by using the field survey data. As mentioned in the methodology section, the study was carried out entirely based on primary data from the four villages of Aranthangi taluk which come under Pudukkottai district of Tamil Nadu in India. For the purpose of the analysis, three villages were selected on the basis of irrigation sources and one village was selected as rainfed village. A total of four villages were selected for the analysis. Of the four villages selected, Ayangudi was considered as the Groundwater Irrigated Village (GIV), Kalakudi was a sample for Canal Irrigated Village (CIV), Kulattur for Tank Irrigated Village (TIV) and Veeramangalam was taken as Rainfed Village (RFV). Both descriptive and regression analyses were used to study the relationship between irrigation and rural poverty.

7.2. Characteristics of Sample Villages

To study the impact of sources-wise irrigation on rural poverty, four villages were selected from Aranthangi taluk in Pudukkottai district of Tamil Nadu. Pudukkottai district is composed of two revenue divisions and nine taluks. Aranthangi is both revenue division and taluk. Aranthangi is the only town in Aranthangi taluk. Therefore, distance from each village is more or less equal to Aranthangi town. The distance from Ayangudi (GIV) to Aranthangi town is 12 kms. similarly, from Kalakudi (CIV) 12 kms. Kulattur (TIV) 10 kms. and Veeramangalam (RFV) 12 kms. from Aranthangi town. The average distance from four villages to Aranthangi is 11 kms., which is almost equal to the distance of each village to Aranthangi town (*see*, Table 7.1). This means that the influence of Aranthangi town on the four selected villages is more or less the same in terms of demographic and socio-economic conditions.

Table 7.1: Particulars of Sample Households

Name of the Sample Village	*Village Type*	*Distance from Town (km.)*	*No. of Sample HHs Selected*	*Total Population of the Selected HHs.*
Ayangudi	Groundwater Irrigated Village (GIV)	12	50	232
Kalakudi	Canal Irrigated Village (CIV)	12	50	218
Kulattur	Tank Irrigated Village (TIV)	10	50	225
Veeramangalam	Rainfed Village (RFV)	12	50	236
Total		**46**	**200**	**911**

Source: Computed using field survey data.

The number of sample households selected from each village was 50. As per the survey, the sample population of Veeramangalam (RFV) was 236, whereas the sample population of Kulattur (TIV) was 225, the sample population of Kalakudi village (CIV) was 218 and the sample population of Ayangudi village (GIV) was 232. The total sample population of four villages was 911 from 200 sample households (*see*, Table 7.1). This means that Veeramangalam represents highest population among the selected villages. This means that the average size of the households was 4.56 per household (see, Table 7.2).

Table 7.2 presents the demographic characteristics of the households. The average age of the respondents was more or less the

Table 7.2: Demographic Characteristics of Sample Households

Variables	*Description of Variables*	*Unit*	*Village Type*				
			GIV	*CIV*	*TIV*	*RFV*	*All*
AGE	Average Age of the Respondent	Year	47.78 (10.81)	48.42 (11.13)	44.00 (12.64)	47.09 (12.09)	46.80 (11.78)
LITE	Literacy Rate	%	82.83 (0.62)	70.35 (0.70)	75.62 (0.89)	77.34 (0.72)	76.53 (0.19)
FS	Average Family Size	No.	4.64 (1.41)	4.36 (1.38)	4.50 (1.63)	4.72 (1.60)	4.56 (1.51)
DR	Dependency ratio	%	40.52 (20.96)	37.61 (20.29)	43.56 (23.32)	49.58 (17.94)	42.92 (21.18)

Note: Values in the brackets are Standard Deviation; GIV: Groundwater irrigated village; CIV: Canal irrigated village: TIV: Tank irrigated village; RFV: Rainfed village.

Source: Same as in Table 7.1.

same in all the four selected villages, ranging from 40 to 48. This shows that majority of agricultural labourers from four villages were above 45 years. Regarding literacy rate, among the four villages, while the population of GIV was more educated, CIV recorded less literate population. The average family size (FS) of GIV (4.64), CIV (4.36), TIV (4.50) and RFV (4.72) were almost equal to the average FS of four villages (4.56). While the dependency ratio (DR) was low in GIV (40.52), the DR of the RFV was very high (49.58). DR of TIV and RFV were above the average DR (42.92) of four villages and the DR of GIV and CIV were below the average DR of four villages. This shows that DR was high in RFV and TIV (*see*, Table 7.2).

7.3. Estimation of Poverty

Although poverty is a multi-dimensional concept, it is crucial to understand how the poverty line in India is being fixed. As pointed out by Tendulkar Committee (Planning Commission, 2013), the concept of poverty is associated with socially perceived deprivation with respect to basic human needs. But, due to variation of basic needs across time and space, the poverty lines also vary, depending upon the level of socio-economic development, social norms and values within regions in a country or cross countries (Hussain *et al.*, 2006). Therefore, the Planning Commission is periodically revising the poverty line to measure the poverty ratio of India from time-to-time.

The first Director General of FAO was the first person to propound the Starvation Line in 1945 which referred to the consumption of less than 2300 calories per person per day. This idea has been transformed into poverty line. By adopting this idea, the Planning Commission of India has defined poverty line on the basis of recommended nutritional requirements of 2400 calories per person per day for rural areas and 2100 calories per person per day for urban areas. This led to income criterion being adopted in India to determine the poverty line.

Before 2004-05, population under poverty was estimated in India mainly based on expenditure on food items, but UNDP in their report of 1990 specifically mentioned that lack of income for measuring absolute poverty is not sufficient reason as minimum income does not lead to basic survival needs and for the standard of living. For the first time, concepts like Uniform Recall Period (URP) and Mixed Recall Period (MRP) were introduced in 2004-05 to determine below poverty line population in India.

The URP and MRP are based on consumer expenditure data, both for food and non-food items. In the case of URP, consumer expenditure data for all the items were collected from a 30-day recall period. On the other hand, MRP data included both food and non-food items. For MRP, consumer expenditure data for five non-food items, namely, clothing, footwear, durable goods, education and institutional medical expenses were collected from a 365-day recall period and the consumption data for the remaining items were collected from a 30-day recall period. Thus, Monthly Per Capita Consumption Expenditure (MPCE) is computed on the basis of three different concepts such as: (1) Uniform Reference Period (URP), (2) Mixed Reference Period (MRP), and (3) Modified Mixed Reference Period (MMRP). As per the Tendulkar Methodology, the poverty line has been expressed in terms of MPCE, based on Mixed Reference Period.

Presently, according to the Tendulkar Methodology, poverty line has been based on Monthly Per Capita Consumption Expenditure (MPCE). The latest consumption criterion to determine poverty line in India is based on 2011-12 data. The poverty line for rural and urban India, for a person per month, are Rs. 816 and 1,000 respectively (Planning Commission, 2013). However, in Tamil Nadu, the poverty line for urban area is Rs. 937 and for rural area, it is Rs. 880.

Since the Tendukar Committee has used consumption expenditure data (2011-12) to estimate poverty, this study has also taken consumption expenditure of the agricultural labourers to estimate poverty.

First of all, Monthly Per Capita Consumption Expenditure (MPCE) has been estimated by dividing total consumption expenditure of sample households by the total population of each household. Secondly, Monthly Per Capita Consumption Expenditures (MPCEs) are arranged in an ascending order. Thirdly, according to the rural poverty line (Rs. 880) of Tamil Nadu (2011-12), the MPCEs which are higher than Rs. 880 or equal to Rs. 880 are regarded as above the poverty line and those MPCEs which are below the consumption line of Rs. 880 are regarded as below the poverty line. This method of calculating rural poverty was used equally for all four sample villages which were selected for the study. Thus, based on the rural poverty line of Tamil Nadu (2011-12), two types of poverty such as PHBPL (Percentage of Household Below Poverty Line) and PPBPL (Percentage of Population Below Poverty Line) were considered for the analysis.

7.4. Description of Variables Used for the Analysis

Many factors determine the level of rural poverty, which are expected to change from one region to another. However, the study had identified only eight variables for the analysis which are also most relevant in determining rural poverty. The variables considered were WRAL, AED, DR, FS, MPCE, MPI, PFWTWI and PNFWTWI (see, Table 7.3).

These variables were assumed to influence the rural poverty (PHBPL and PPBPL). Therefore, PHBPL and PPBPL were considered as the dependent variables separately in each regression analysis by keeping all other variables as independent variables. Since the main aim of the study was to find out the relationship between irrigation and rural poverty among different types of villages, dummy variable was used in the place of irrigation variable.

Wage Rate of Agricultural Labourer (WRAL) is defined as the average wage rate per day for male and female. It explains the income of the households. Average Employment Days (AED) stands for employment opportunities for the people. Dependency Ratio (DR) indicates how many people were depending on the working population in the sample households. If dependent people were more than that of the working population, it shows that poverty must be existing in those households. MPCE is an important variable which is used to estimate poverty in India. If the MPCE is lower than the State rural poverty line fixed by the Planning Commission (2013), it is regarded that they are under the poverty line. Monthly Per Capita Income (MPI) is another important variable for poverty estimation, because MPCE normally depends on income. The two variables viz., Percentage of Farm Wage to Total Wage Income (PFWTWI) and Percentage of Non-Farm Wage to Total Wage Income (PNFWTWI) were also included for the analysis to understand which of the two variables was more pronounced in determining poverty.

As underlined elsewhere in the study, the main objective of the study was to find out which of the irrigation source played a significant role in reducing rural poverty. Therefore, first of all, the variables at the source-wise irrigated villages were investigated. The average Wage Rate of Agricultural Labourer (WRAL) of all four villages was around Rs. 245.00, which was more or less the same to the WRAL of GIV, CIV, TIV and RFV. This shows that agriculture wage rate was the same for all those who worked in agriculture (see, Table 7.3). The average employment days of GIV, CIV, TIV and RFV were 19.19 days, 16.26 days, 11.69 days and 10.68 days respectively. While Ayangudi (GIV) recorded the highest employment days for a month, Veeramangalam (RFV) recorded the lowest employment days. It shows that GIV provided more employment opportunities, followed by CIV, TIV and RFV. RFV and TIV recorded employment days, which were below the total average employment days of 14.61 per month.

While the average dependency ratio was 42.92, average family size was 4.56. The average monthly per capita expenditure was about Rs. 1047.00 and per capita income was around Rs. 1438.00 of four villages. Monthly per capita expenditure of GIV and CIV was above the total average, but rainfed village was below the total average, followed by the TIV. The same situation was witnessed in monthly income of the villages. By expenditure and income, it can be inferred that rainfed village recorded the highest number of poor people, followed by tank irrigated village, canal irrigated village and groundwater irrigated village.

The average of Percentage of Farm Wage to total Wage Income (PFWTWI) was 58.09 per cent and Percentage of Non-Farm Wage to total Wage Income (PNFWTWI) was 41.91 per cent. Percentage

Table 7.3: Description of the Variables used for Field Data Analysis

Variables	*Description of Variables*	*Unit*	*Village Type*				
			GIV	*CIV*	*TIV*	*RFV*	*All*
AFS	Average Family Size	N	4.64 (1.41)	4.36 (1.38)	4.50 (1.63)	4.72 (1.60)	4.56 (1.51)
DR	Dependency ratio	%	40.52 (20.96)	37.61 (20.29)	43.56 (23.32)	49.58 (17.94)	42.92 (21.18)
AWRAL	Average Wage Rate of Agricultural Labourer	Rs./ day	230.00 (59.29)	233.00 (42.40)	239.00 (108.04)	279.00 (110.78)	245.00 (88.75)
AED	Average Employment Days	Days/ month	19.19 (4.44)	16.26 (4.81)	11.69 (3.69)	10.68 (12.07)	14.61 (5.45)
MPCE	Monthly Per Capita Expenditure	Rs.	1290.00 (406.04)	1160.00 (439.05)	930.00 (239.05)	816.00 (210.66)	1047.00 (387.89)
MPI	Monthly Per Capita Income	Rs.	2005.00 (799.93)	1779.00 (633.06)	1141.00 (554.20)	849.00 (342.96)	1438.00 (772.29)
PFWTWI	Percentage of Farm Wage to Total Wage Income	%	65.63 (12.26)	59.72 (15.56)	55.76 (14.16)	51.46 (15.26)	58.09 (15.01)
PNFWTWI	Percentage of Non-Farm Wage to Total Wage Income	%	34.37 (12.26)	40.28 (15.56)	44.24 (14.16)	48.54 (15.26)	41.91 (15.01
PHBPL	Percentage of Household Below Poverty Line	%	22.00 (0.84)	34.00 (0.96	48.00 (1.01)	60.00 (0.99)	41.00 (0.99)
PPBPL	Percentage of Population Below Poverty Line	%	27.16 (41.85)	37.16 (48.68)	53.78 (49.99)	63.98 (49.49)	45.66 (49.30)

Note: Values in the brackets are Standard Deviation.
Source: Same as in Table 7.1.

of Household below Poverty Line (PHBPL) was 22 in GIV, 34 in CIV, 48 in TIV and 60 in RFV. Similarly, Percentage of Population Below Poverty Line (PPBPL) was 27.16 for GIV, 37.16 for CIV, 53.78 for TIV and 63.98 for RFV. In both PHBPL and PPBPL cases, GIV recorded a lower poverty ratio than CIV, Canal Irrigated Villages (CIV) recorded less poverty ratio than the TIV and finally, Tank Irrigated Village (TIV) recorded less poverty ratio than RFV. Therefore, it can be concluded that poverty ratio was the highest in rainfed area and then comparatively lesser in tank, canal and groundwater irrigated areas. However, one cannot clearly say on the basis of this information that groundwater irrigated area has less poor than that of rainfed area. In order to find out the significance of each source of irrigation on rural poverty, a detailed regression analysis was carried out.

Two types of regression analysis were performed to explain the relationship between source-wise irrigation and rural poverty. To establish the independent relationship between source-wise irrigation and rural poverty, different types of simple regressions were used, without considering any other poverty determining variable. The simple regressions were used to study the variation of PPBPL within source-wise irrigated villages, between irrigated village and un-irrigated village, and also how the irrigation was responsible for reducing rural poverty. The different types of regression equations estimated were:

$$PPBPL = \alpha + b_1 D_i + e_i \quad \ldots (12)$$

Where,

PPBPL = percentage of population below poverty line,
D_i = irrigation dummy (GIV=1 and CIV=0),
b_1 = regression parameter to be estimated,
α = constant,
e_i = error term.

$$PPBPL = \alpha + b_1 D_i + e_i \quad \ldots (13)$$

{D_i = irrigation dummy (GIV=1 and TIV=0)}

$$PPBPL = \alpha + b_1 D_i + e_i \quad \ldots (14)$$

{D_i = irrigation dummy (CIV=1 and TIV=0)}

$$PPBPL = \alpha + b_1 D_i + e_i \quad \ldots (15)$$

{D_i = irrigation dummy (GIV=1and RFV=0)}

$$PPBPL = \alpha + b_1 D_i + e_i \quad \ldots (16)$$

{D_i = irrigation dummy (CIV=1 and RFV=0)}

$$PPBPL = \alpha + b_1 D_i + e_i \quad \ldots (17)$$

{D_i = irrigation dummy (TIV=1 and RFV=0)}

$$PPBPL = \alpha + b_1 D_i + e_i \quad \ldots (18)$$

{D_i = irrigation dummy (GIV=3, CIV=2, TIV=1 and RFV=0)}

After analysing independent relationships among source-wise

irrigation and rural poverty, multiple regression analysis was performed because it is a known fact that rural poverty is determined by several factors. It was also essential to carry out multiple regression analysis to understand as to which of the selected poverty determinant variables was playing a major role in influencing the rural poverty. Therefore, multiple regression was used, by considering PPBPL as the dependent variable and other poverty determinant variables as independent variables. The multiple regression model used for the analysis was as follows:

$$PPBPL = \alpha + b_1 AED + b_2 DR + b_3 FS + b_4 MPI + b_5 PNFWTWI + b_6 WRAL + b_7 D_i + e_i \quad \ldots (19)$$

Where,

PPBPL = percentage of population below poverty line
AED = average employment days/month/person
DR = dependency ratio (%)
FS = family size (number of person)
MPI = monthly per capita income (Rs.)
PNFWTWI = percentage of non-farm wage to total wage income
WRAL = wage rate of agricultural labourers/day
D_i = irrigation dummy (GIV=3, CIV=2, TIV=1 and RFV=0)
b_1 = regression parameter to be estimated
α = constant
e_i = error term.

Thus, the analyses were carried out with the expectation that the selected variables would greatly and significantly influence the rural poverty.

7.5. Employment, Income and Expenditure of Sample Households

There is a general thinking that irrigation increases agricultural production and productivity, increases cropping intensity, enhances employment and income, and finally, helps to increase the purchasing power of poor. Before studying the relationship between irrigation and rural poverty in the selected villages using regression analysis, employment, income and expenditure pattern of the sample households selected for the analysis should be studied.

Table 7.4 provides details of employment of the sample households. The agricultural labourers of Ayangudi which was a Groundwater Irrigated Village (GIV) obtained about 16 days of farm work and seven days of non-farm work per month. The total employment days for the same village were 20 days per month. Equally, agricultural labourers of Kalakudi, a Canal Irrigated Village (CIV) could manage around 17 days of work per month. The agricultural labourers of Kulattur, a Tank Irrigated Village (TIV) could get 12 days of work per month and agricultural labourers of Veeramangalam, a Rainfed Village (RFV) obtained 10 days of work, which were below the average employment days of agricultural labourers for four villages. Many studies showed that increased employment days would improve income and better the standard of living. It is understood from the data shown in Table 7.4 that the living standard of people in GIV was better than CIV, CIV was better comparatively than TIV and TIV was better than RFV. On the whole, as expected, tank and rainfed villages provided less employment opportunities to the labour households.

Table 7.4: Employment Days of Sample Households

(*Day/month/person*)

Village Type	*AFED*	*ANFED*	*AED*
GIV	15.57 (81.16)	6.64 (34.60)	19.19 (100)
CIV	12.06 (74.16)	7.82 (48.08)	16.26 (100)
TIV	6.19 (52.94)	8.82 (75.42)	11.69 (100)
RFV	3.38 (31.64)	9.18 (85.92)	10.68 (100)
Total	**9.57** **(65.52)**	**8.70** **(59.57)**	**14.61** **(100)**

Notes: Values in the brackets are percentage; AFED: Average farm employment days; ANFED: Average non-farm employment days; AED: Average employment days.

Source: Same as in Table 7.1.

Both Table 7.4 and Figure 7.1 indicate that agricultural labourers belonging to GIV obtained more employment days than their counterparts in CIV, TIV and RFV, while agricultural labourers of CIV obtained more employment days than labourers in TIV and RFV.

Agricultural labourers of TIV recorded more employment days than labourers of RFV. It can also be pointed out from the data that the employment days of TIV and RFV registered more or less the same trend. It means that the living standards of these two villages were more or less the same, which were lower than the other two villages with groundwater and canal irrigation.

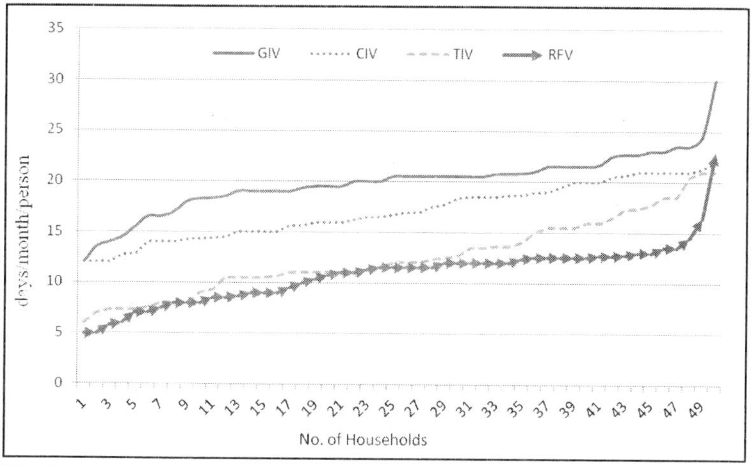

Fig. 7.1: Trends in Employment Days of Sample Households across Selected Villages

Source: Field Survey.

Similar to the employment days, income is also very important in determining the living standard or the poverty situation of the villages. The monthly per capita income of agricultural labourers of GIV, CIV, TIV and RFV were around Rs. 2005.00, Rs. 1779.00, Rs. 1141.00 and Rs. 849.00 respectively (see, Table 7.5). The monthly per capita income is a mixture of farm income and non-farm income. Not surprisingly, the farm income of agricultural labourers in GIV was higher than the farm income of agricultural labourers of other villages such as CIV, TIV and RFV. Further, monthly per capita farm income of agricultural labourers in CIV was higher than the farm income of agricultural labourers of TIV and RFV. In addition, monthly per capita farm income of agricultural labourers in TIV was higher as compared to the farm income of agricultural labourers of RFV. This means that the farm labourers of GIV regions reported better livelihood opportunities than labourers in CIV, TIV and RFV. This is expected because the employment opportunities are better in the assured irrigated villages.

Table 7.5: Monthly Income of Sample Households

(*Rs./person*)

Village Type	*MPFI*	*MPNFI*	*MPI*
GIV	1449.00 (72.29)	556.00 (27.71)	2005.00 (100)
CIV	1156.00 (64.96)	623.00 (35.04)	1779.00 (100)
TIV	590.00 (51.73)	551.00 (48.27)	1141.00 (100)
RFV	334.00 (39.40)	515.00 (60.60)	849.00 (100)
Total	**878.00** **(61.06)**	**560.00** **(38.94)**	**1438.00** **(100)**

Note: Values in the brackets are percentage; MPFI: Monthly per capita farm income; MPNFI: Monthly per capita non-farm income; MPI: Monthly per capita income.

Sources: Same as in Table 7.1.

Figure 7.2 also demonstrates that the agricultural labourers of GIV recorded more per capita income. The agricultural labourers of CIV obtained less income than that of GIV. However, income trends of agricultural labourers of TIV and RFV indicated upward trend with less variation. This means that there was no significant difference in income between TIV and RFV.

Following the Tendulkar Methodology, Monthly Per Capita Consumption Expenditure (MPCE) was taken for poverty measurement. The analysis of data reveals that MPCE of agriculture labourers was about Rs. 1289.00 in GIV, Rs. 1160.00 in CIV, Rs. 930.00 in TIV and Rs. 816.00 in RFV. MPCE was found high in GIV and low in RFV (see, Table 7.6). This shows that MPCE of agricultural labourers belonging to GIV was greater than in CIV, CIV was greater than TIV and TIV was greater than RFV. It reveals that more people may live under below poverty line in rainfed villages than other villages, which is also expected.

Figure 7.3 also clearly shows that the MPCE trend line of GIV was higher and MPCE trend line of CIV was just below the GIV trend line followed by TIV and RFV. This means that living standard of the people in GIV was the best followed by CIV, TIV and RFV.

However, the level of rural poverty in different villages cannot be studied only by analysing employment, consumption, expenditure etc. Therefore, to find out the exact level of poverty in all the four

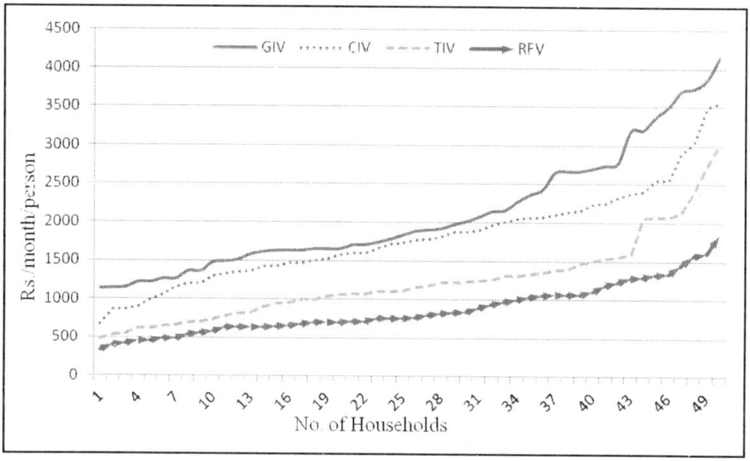

Fig. 7.2: Trends in Monthly Income of Sample Households across Selected Villages

Source: Same as in Table 7.1.

Table 7.6: Monthly Consumption Expenditure of Sample Households

(Rs./person)

Village Type	*MPCE on Food items*	*MPCE on Non-Food items*	*MPCE on total Items*
GIV	745.00 (57.74)	545.00 (42.26)	1290.00 (100)
CIV	664.00 (57.22)	496.00 (42.76)	1160.00 (100)
TIV	591.00 (63.54)	339.00 (36.46)	930.00 (100)
RFV	533.50 (65.42)	282.00 (34.58)	816.00 (100)
Total	**633.00** **(60.43)**	**414.00** **(39.58)**	**1047.00** **(100)**

Note: Figure in brackets is percentage.

Source: Same as in Table 7.1.

types of villages, both PPBPL (Percentage of Population Below Poverty Line) and PHBPL (Percentage of Household Below Poverty Line) were estimated by following the Tendulkar Methodology (Planning Commission, 2013).

Table 7.7 presents the level of poverty both in terms of number of households and number of population. It is clear that households living below poverty line were less in groundwater irrigated village

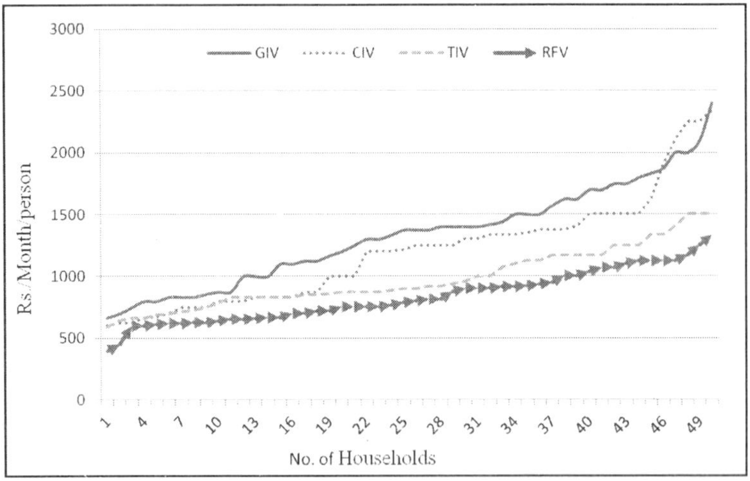

Fig. 7.3: Trends in Monthly Expenditure on Consumption across Selected Villages

Source: Same as in Table 7.1.

Tables 7.7: Number and Percentage of Sample Households, and Population Below Poverty Line

Village Type	*NHBPL*	*NPBPL*	*PHBPL*	*PPBPL*
GIV	11	63	22.00	27.16
CIV	17	81	34.00	37.16
TIV	24	121	48.00	53.78
RFV	30	151	60.00	63.98
Total	**82**	**416**	**41.00**	**45.66**

Note: NHBPL: Number of households below poverty line; NPBPL: Number of population below poverty line; PHBPL: Percentage of households below poverty line; PPBPL: Percentage of population below poverty line.

Source: Same as in Table 7.1.

compared to all other villages taken for the analysis. As GIV has assured irrigation, which provides better employment opportunities, most agricultural labourers were able to cross poverty line. This was not possible in tank and rainfed villages because of poor irrigation facility. It is clear that NHBPL, PHBPL, NPPBPL and PPBPL were more in RFV and very less in GIV sample area, which is expected in this study.

In conclusion, the above analysis confirms that assured irrigation facility is the effective factor in rural poverty reduction. This is possible because irrigation increases cropping intensity and landuse intensity both of which help to increase production and productivity of crops, gives employment opportunities (year-round) and raises the living standard of the agriculture labourers. However, one may not be able to strongly assert the extent of impact of irrigation on the rural poverty only through descriptive analysis. Therefore, in order to find out the magnitude of impact of different sources of irrigation on rural poverty, different types of simple and multiple regressions were estimated, as explained in the methodology section. This analysis is expected to identify which of the irrigation sources played a pivotal role in determining rural poverty and also which of the poverty determining variables was significantly and predominantly influencing the rural poverty reduction. The regression results are discussed in detail in the following sections.

7.6. Source-wise Irrigation and Poverty Nexus

It is very well understood from the above analysis that the GIV (Ayangudi) recorded less number of poor families and poor people as compared to CIV (Kalakudi). Likewise, with regard to poor households and poor people, CIV was better than TIV (Kulattur) and finally, TIV recorded less poor households and poor people than RFV (Veeramangalam). This shows that RFV had more poor households and more number of poor people. The major factors, which determined the rural poverty like employment days, monthly per capita income and monthly per capita consumption expenditure were less in rainfed village than in the irrigated villages. On the whole, it is clear from the analysis that irrigation played a major role in poverty determination. However, one cannot identify from the above information the variable which made a difference in poverty reduction. Keeping this scenario in view, an attempt had been made here to capture the factors that influenced the percentage of population below poverty line.

Two types of regression analyses were employed to explain the relationship between source-wise irrigation and the rural poverty. To establish the independent relationship between source-wise irrigation and rural poverty, different types of simple regressions were used, without considering any other poverty determining variables. Simple regressions were used to study the variation in PPBPL within source-wise irrigated villages, between irrigated village and un-irrigated village. In order to represent the irrigation variable in the regression analysis, D_i (DUMMY) variable was included as the irrigation variable.

Table 7.8 provides the results of regression (equation 12) estimated by treating PPBPL as a dependent variable and D_i (irrigation dummy) as an independent variable. This was done to examine the variation of poverty between Groundwater Irrigated Village (GIV) and Canal Irrigated Village (CIV). The regression coefficient of irrigation (dummy) was significant and negative. This shows that groundwater irrigation was more pronounced in terms of determining the rural poverty as compared to canal irrigation.

Table 7.8: Simple Linear Regression Results–Groundwater Irrigation *versus* Canal Irrigation

Variable	*Model No. (12)*
DUMMY (GIV=1, CIV=0)	–12.500[d] (–1.377)
Constant	34.500[a] (5.374)
R^2	0.019
Adjusted R^2	0.009
D.W.	1.938
F	1.896
N	100

Note: Figures in the brackets are 't' value; a and d are significant level at 1 and 20 per cent respectively.

Source: Same as in Table 7.1.

The results of equation (13) are presented in Table 7.9. The regression was computed by using PPBPL as the dependent variable and irrigation dummy (GIV=1, TIV=0) as an independent variable. It examined the variation of poverty in groundwater irrigated village *versus* tank irrigated village. The results of regression showed that irrigation dummy did significantly and negatively influence the rural poverty. It pointed out that groundwater irrigation played a pivotal role in reducing rural poverty as compared to the tank irrigation. The regression coefficient also demonstrated that the strength of impact of groundwater on poverty was much better as compared to result estimated between groundwater and canal irrigation.

Table 7.9: Simple Linear Regression Results–Groundwater Irrigation *versus* Tank Irrigation

Variable	*Model No. (13)*
DUMMY (GIV=1, TIV=0)	–23.600[a]
	(–2.560)
Constant	45.600[a]
	(6.995)
R^2	0.063
Adjusted R^2	0.053
D.W.	1.905
F	6.553
N	100

Note: Figures in the brackets are 't' value; a is significant level at 1 per cent.
Sources: Same as in Table 7.1.

The results of regression analysis carried out to examine the variation of poverty between CIV and TIV are presented in Table 7.10 (equation 14). This showed that canal irrigation was better than the tank irrigation in reducing the rural poverty.

Table 7.11 (equation 15) represents the regression results of GIV with RFV in terms of determining the rural poverty. In this regression, PPBPL was considered as the dependent variable and D_i (irrigation dummy) as an independent variable to examine the variation of poverty between GIV and RFV. The result of the regression showed that the coefficient of irrigation was highly significant and negative. It demonstrated that the role of groundwater irrigation in reducing the

Table 7.10: Simple Linear Regression Results–Canal Irrigation *versus* Tank Irrigation

Variable	*Model No. (14)*
DUMMY (CIV=1, TIV=0)	–11.100[ns]
	(–1 125)
Constant	45.600[a]
	(6.535)
R^2	0.013
Adjusted R^2	0.003
D.W.	2.138
F	1.267
N	100

Note: Figures in the brackets are't' value; a is significant level at 1 per cent; ns—not significant.
Source: Same as in Table 7.1.

Table 7.11: Simple Linear Regression Results–Groundwater Irrigation *versus* Rainfed

Variable	Model No. (15)
DUMMY (GIV=1, RFV=0)	–38.000[a] (–4.146)
Constant	60.000[a] (9.258)
R^2	0.149
Adjusted R^2	0.141
D.W.	2.048
F	17.190
N	100

Notes: Figures in the brackets are 't' value; a is significant level at 1 per cent.
Source: Same as in Table 7.1.

rural poverty was remarkable as compared to rainfed. The value of R^2 was found to be 0.149, indicating that 14 per cent of the variation in rural poverty was explained by the groundwater irrigation alone.

Following the above analysis, separate regression was also estimated to study the impact of canal irrigation on rural poverty in relation to rainfed areas. The regression results in Table 7.12 (equation 16) show the significant role of canal irrigation in alleviating rural poverty as compared to rainfed area.

Table 7.12: Simple Linear Regression Results–Canal Irrigation *versus* Rainfed

Variable	Model No. (16)
DUMMY (CIV=1, RFV=0)	–25.500[a] (2.598)
Constant	60.000[a] (8.644)
R^2	0.064
Adjusted R^2	0.055
D.W.	2.253
F	6.747
N	100

Note: Figures in the brackets are 't' value; a is significant level at 1 per cent.
Source: Same as in Table 7.1.

Table 7.13 (results of equation 17) displays the regression results estimated between Tank Irrigated Village (TIV) and Rainfed Village (RFV). The explanatory variable of irrigation was used as DUMMY variable, where TIV=1 and RFV= 0. The result pointed out that tank

Table 7.13: Simple Linear Regression Results–Tank Irrigation *versus* Rainfed

Variable	*Model No. (17)*
DUMMY (TIV=1, RFV=0)	–14.400[a] (–1.448)
Constant	60.000[a] (8.530)
R^2	0.021
Adjusted R^2	0.011
D.W.	2.190
F	2.096
N	100

Note: Figures in the brackets are 't' value; a is significant at 1 per cent level.
Source: Same as in Table 7.1.

irrigation inversely and significantly influenced the rural poverty. However, the role of tank irrigation on rural poverty alleviation was relatively less compared to canal irrigation and groundwater irrigation.

7.7. Irrigation and Rural Poverty Nexus

After estimating different types of simple regressions to explain the relation between source-wise irrigation and rural poverty, regressions were computed to establish the relationship between irrigation and rural poverty by treating PPBPL as the dependent variable and irrigation sources as independent variables. The main difference between this analysis and the earlier one is that it used all the four villages (as a dummy variable) in a single equation. This is done specifically to study the average impact of different irrigation sources on the rural poverty reduction.

Table 7.14 (Equation 18) presents the relationship between source-wise irrigation and the rural poverty. In this regression, irrigation sources were considered as the explanatory variable and PPBPL as a dependent variable. The irrigation variable was considered as DUMMY variable (D_i) where GIV=3, CIV=2, TIV=1 and RFV=0 were taken for the analysis. The regression results revealed that there was a strong and significant association between irrigation and rural poverty. This regression coefficient indicated that on an average, when agricultural labourers shift from rainfed to an irrigated village, the poverty can be reduced to the extent of 12.50 per cent. On the whole, as per the results of Table 7.14, there was strong, inverse and significant relationship between irrigation and the rural poverty.

Table 7.14: Simple Linear Regression Results–Irrigation Determines Poverty (PPBPL)

Variable	*Model No. (18)*
DUMMY (GIV=3, CIV=2, TIV=1, RFV=0)	–12.510a (–4.175)
Constant	59.290a (10.576)
R^2	0.081
Adjusted R^2	0.076
D.W.	2.093
F	17.430
N	200

Note: Figures in the brackets are 't' value; [a] is significant at 1 per cent level.
Source: Same as in Table 7.1.

Besides irrigation factors, many other factors play a role in determining the rural poverty. Therefore, following the analysis of independent relationships between irrigation and rural poverty, multiple regression analysis was performed to understand which of the selected poverty determinant variables played a major role in influencing rural poverty. Keeping this in view, multiple regression was estimated by treating PPBPL as the dependent variable and other variables (AED, DR, FS, MPI, PNFWTWI, WRAL and D_i) as independent variables, to identify which of the poverty determinant variables was significantly associated with rural poverty (see, Table 7.15). In order to include irrigation variable in the regression (equation 19), DUMMY variable (D_i) was considered where GIV=3, CIV=2, TIV=1 and RFV=0.

The results presented in Table 7.15 revealed that the regression coefficient of non-farm income (PNFWTWI) was significantly negative which indicated that an increase in PNFWTWI resulted in the decrease of the rural poverty. The coefficient of MPI turned out to be negative but not significant, implying the fact that MPI played a lesser role in determining the rural poverty. Coefficient of WRAL turned out to be negative but not significant. This revealed that this variable played a lesser role in determining the rural poverty. The regression coefficient of dependency ratio (DR) was found to be significantly positive. This revealed that with an increase in DR, poverty ratio will also increase in the sample area. The regression equation (19) of family size (FS) turned out be significant, but not negative, showing that there was not much effect of FS on poverty reduction.

Table 7.15: Multivariate Regression Results–Factors Determining Poverty (PPBPL)

Variables	*Model No.* (19)
WRAL	–0.024[ns] (1.223)
AED	0.509[ns] (–0.533)
DR	0.764[a] (0.587)
FS	5.661[a] (2.582)
MPI	–0.010[ns] (2.458)
PNFWTWI	–0.291[d] (–1.092)
DUMMY (GIV=3, CIV=2, TIV=1, RFV=0)	–8.74[a] (–1.283)
Constant	21.758[ns] (–1.902)
R^2	0.336
Adjusted R^2	0.312
D.W.	1.891
F	13.891
N	200

Note: Figures in the brackets are 't' value; a and d are significant at 1 and 20 per cent level respectively; ns—not significant.

Source: Same as in Table 7.1.

Unlike the other variables included in the regression analysis, the coefficient of irrigation dummy was found to be significantly negative. This implies that among the poverty determinant factors, irrigation helped significantly in reducing the rural poverty. In addition, among the variables included in the regression estimation, the magnitude of irrigation (dummy) coefficient was the largest. On the whole, the results of the regression (*see*, Table 7.15) demonstrated that among the six variables included in equation (19), irrigation variable (DUMMY) significantly determined the rural poverty. The results of regression also indicated that irrigation was the major factor in reducing poverty in the selected villages.

7.8. Conclusion

The major aim of the field data based study was to analyse the impact of source-wise irrigation on poverty reduction. Both descriptive and regression analysis were carried out for the analysis. The descriptive analysis revealed that percentage of population below poverty line was found to be higher in RFV (Veeramangalam) but comparatively less in TIV (Kulattur), followed by CIV (Kalakudi) and GIV (Ayangudi). This analysis revealed that the capacity of groundwater irrigation was high in reducing rural poverty as compared to canal irrigation. It is also found out that the impact of canal irrigation on reduction of rural poverty was better than the tank irrigation. Further, the study demonstrated (not only from descriptive analysis, but also, from the simple and multiple regression analysis) that among the variables included for the analysis, groundwater irrigation significantly determined the rural poverty as compared to other sources of irrigation. Next to the groundwater irrigation, the impact of canal irrigation was remarkable on reducing rural poverty. Though the tank irrigated area performed better than the rainfed areas, tank's impact on reducing the rural poverty seems to be very low as compared to other sources of irrigation. On the whole, irrigation variable appears to be the dominant and crucial factor in influencing or determining the rural poverty in the selected villages.

8

Findings and Recommendations

8.1. Introduction

After having analysed the relationship between irrigation and rural poverty by using State and district-wise data as well as field-level data collected from four locations, we present findings and recommendations of the study in this chapter. Although irrigation has been recognised as a crucial factor in explaining the growth in agriculture and rural economy in the literature, it has not been used as one of the principal explanatory variables in the poverty-related studies in India until 2001. Only a few studies are available relating irrigation development to the agricultural growth. But very limited studies are available relating irrigation development to the rural poverty by using data from 1973-74 to 2011-12 covering various States in India. In fact, no study is available covering district-level data on the nexus between irrigation and rural poverty. To our knowledge, studies are also not at all available relating source-wise irrigation to the rural poverty by using field survey data. Keeping this in view, an attempt has been made in this study to measure the relationship between irrigation and rural poverty by using both macro- and micro-level data.

8.2. Objectives

The main objectives of the study are:

1. To study the relationship between irrigation development and the rural poverty across the major States in India, from 1973-74 to 2011-12.
2. To analyse the impact of irrigation on rural poverty across the districts in India.

3. To study the relationship between base-level irrigation and rural poverty.
4. To analyse the impact ot source-wise irrigation on rural poverty utilising the field survey data.

8.3. Method and Data

The present study on irrigation and rural poverty was carried out using both macro- and micro-level data. The macro-level analysis was conducted using secondary data collected from both State and district-level across India. The micro-level analysis was conducted using primary data collected from four locations in Pudukkottai district, Tamil Nadu State. Since the main objective of the study was to analyse the nexus between irrigation and rural poverty, the Percentage of Rural population below the Poverty line (PRP) data, released by the Planning Commission for eight different time points, namely 1973-74, 1977-78, 1983, 1987-88, 1993-94, 1999-2000, 2004-05 and 2011-12, have been used as the main data source for the State-level analysis (Planning Commission, 2014). The other variables, considered for the analysis are GIAGCA, IAPTRP RWAL, PFG, SDAPHRP, CI and FPHRP. These data were collected and compiled from sources like Indian Agricultural Statistics, Area and Production of Principal Crops in India, Agricultural Wages in India (published by the Ministry of Agriculture, Government of India, New Delhi), Census of India (GoI, various years) and also from some of the recent published materials.

Similarly, for the district-level analysis, data on Percentage of Rural Poverty (PRP) for the year 2004-05 were collected from Choudhuri and Gupta (2009) and the other poverty determining variables like GIAGCA, GCAPTRP, LITE, ROAD, ELEC and WRAL were collected and compiled from various issues of Indian Agricultural Statistics, published by the Ministry of Agriculture, Government of India, New Delhi, Bhalla and Singh (2010, 2012), Census of India (GoI, 1971, 1981, 1991) and Agriculture wages in India (various years).

As the main aim of the micro-level study was to find out the importance of source-wise irrigation on rural poverty, primary data for the period 2013-14 were collected from four villages, namely Ayangudi (groundwater irrigated village), Kalakudi (canal irrigated village), Kulattur (tank irrigated village) and Veeramangalam (rainfed village). These villages were selected from Aranthangi taluk, Pudukkottai district, Tamil Nadu State, India. Two prime variables, namely Percentage of Households Below Poverty Line (PHBPL) and Percentage of Population Below Poverty Line (PPBPL) were regarded as poverty variables in the analysis. The other poverty determinants such as MPCE, WRAL, AED, DR, MPI, PFWTWI and PNFWTWI were included for the analysis. Both descriptive and regression analyses were used to study the nexus between irrigation and rural poverty.

8.4. Findings from State-level Analysis

The descriptive analysis revealed that while the percentage of rural poverty has been declining from 1973-74 to 2011-12, poverty determinant variables (CI, IAPTRP, FPHRP, GIAGCA, PFG, RWAL and SDAPHRP) were increasing during the same period.

The study attempted to find out the incidence of poverty and characteristics of States selected for the analysis by dividing the States into those Above the National Average (ANA) and Below the National Average (BNA), in terms of percentage of population below the poverty line and studied their irrigation-related characteristics at all eight time points: 1973-74, 1977-78, 1983, 1987-88, 1993-94, 1999-2000, 2004-05 and 2011-12. It was found that percentage of population living below poverty in rural areas had declined substantially at the national-level (from 56.44% in 1973-74 to 25.70% in 2011-12). However, the reduction was not the same across the States. While the rate of reduction was significant in States like Andhra Pradesh, Gujarat, Haryana, Karnataka, Madhya Pradesh, Kerala and West Bengal, it was less than the national-level average in other States. With regard to individual States, despite a significant reduction in the level of poverty between 1973-74 and 2011-12, States like Odisha, Bihar, Madhya Pradesh and Uttar Pradesh continued to have a higher percentage of population below the poverty line in 2011-12. In all these States, the level of IAPTRP was lower than the national-level average. The percentage of rural poverty was not only less in the States of Punjab, Haryana, Gujarat, Rajasthan and Tamil Nadu, but also declined significantly between 1973-74 and 2011-12, possibly because of higher IAPTRP. This suggests that IAPRTP (irrigation) played an important role in decreasing the poverty in rural areas.

Correlation value was estimated to understand the association between poverty determinant variables and poverty (PRP). Correlation analysis confirmed the strong and negative relationship between irrigation and rural poverty for eight point times considered for the State-level analysis.

To analyse the impact of irrigation on rural poverty at State-level, simple regression (OLS) was computed by treating irrigation (IAPTRP) as the explanatory variable and poverty as the dependent variable (PRP). Results of independent regression analysis demonstrated that irrigation significantly determines rural poverty at all the eight time points specified earlier.

Development of irrigation cannot make a significant impact instantaneously on rural poverty in any given region and, therefore, it was necessary to use irrigation as a lagged variable in the regression analysis to capture its real impact on rural poverty. Keeping this in view, two different types of regressions were estimated separately, treating irrigation with a five year time lag ($PRP_t = \alpha + b_1 IAPTRP_{t-5}$) and also with 10-year time lag ($PRP_t = \alpha + b_1 IAPTRP_{t-10}$). The results showed that the strength of impact of irrigation on reducing the rural poverty was much better when compared to the regression results computed by treating irrigation without any time lag. This strongly demonstrates that base-level irrigation is also important in reducing the rural poverty.

8.5. District-level Analysis

In the first step of analysis at the district-level, descriptive analysis were carried out to study the characteristics of the poverty determinant variables (CI, ELE, GCAPTRP, GIAGCA, LITE, ROAD and WAGE), expecting that these variables would greatly influence the Percentage of Rural Poverty (PRP) for four points time (1970-71, 1980-81, 1990-91 and 2000-01). The analysis demonstrated that the average and standard deviation of all these variables had increased during the study period implying that these variables did determine the rural poverty.

Districts were categorised into districts Above the Average (AA) and Below the Average (BA) based on district poverty-level, in all four points of time in order to understand the relationship between poverty and poverty determinants variables selected for the analysis. The result showed that among the poverty determinant variables, namely, CI, ELEC, GCAPTRP, GIAGCA, LITE, ROAD and WAGE, the difference between AA and BA districts was more pronounced in GIAGCA (Percentage of Gross Irrigated Area to Gross Cropped Area), in all the four time points. This means that districts, having higher irrigation coverage, experienced lower poverty rate while lower irrigation districts experienced higher poverty rate. This confirmed that there was inverse relationship between irrigation and rural poverty.

Similar to the study of relationship between poverty determinant variables and rural poverty, independent relationship between irrigation and poverty, was also studied by dividing 178 districts into three parts, namely Districts with Severe Poverty (DSP), Districts with Medium Poverty (DMP) and Districts with Lower Poverty (DLP) in relation to level of irrigation. The analysis reveals that rural poverty was severe in districts where GIAGCA was low as compared to districts with medium poverty in all four point times. Districts, with lower poverty recorded better GIAGCA than districts with medium poverty during the same period of time. Irrigation was relatively higher among the districts whose average GIAGCA was below the average GIAGCA of 178 districts than in the case of districts whose GIAGCA was above the average GIAGCA.

In addition to studying the relationship between the GIAGCA (Percentage of Gross Irrigated Area to Gross Cropped Area) and Percentage of Rural Poverty (PRP), an attempt was also made to find out whether the Irrigation Area Per Thousand Rural Population (IAPTRP) was associated with the Percentage of Rural Poverty (PRP) during these periods in 178 districts. It is evident that districts with lower poverty recorded more IAPTRP than districts with medium poverty and severe poverty in all four time points. Districts with high poverty recorded low irrigation (GIAGCA). This demonstrated that irrigation did play a very important role in rural poverty reduction.

After understanding the relationship between irrigation and rural poverty from the descriptive analysis, the independent relationship between irrigation and rural poverty was analysed by treating irrigation (GIAGCA) as the independent variable and rural poverty (PRP) as the dependent variable through a simple regression analysis. As expected, the results of the regression analysis revealed that there was significant and inverse relationship between the two, implying that irrigation significantly determined the rural poverty.

It is known that irrigation benefit flows on certain pathways to finally make an impact on the poor person, which normally takes time. Therefore, it was necessary to use irrigation as a lagged variable in the regression analysis to capture its real impact on rural poverty. Keeping this in view, regression analysis was carried out separately, treating irrigation as a lagged variable with 10, 20 and 30 years. The results show that the strength of impact of irrigation on reducing rural poverty was much better with time lag when compared to the regression results computed by treating irrigation without any time lag. Further, the strength of regression coefficients and the R^2 was also increasing over time when irrigation was used as a lagged variable in the regression analysis. This indicated that there was impact of base level irrigation on reducing rural poverty.

Since poverty is determined by various factors, multiple regression analysis was also carried out in addition to the simple regression in order to find out which of the factors were predominant and significant in determining the rural poverty. Four types of multiple regressions were employed, by keeping PRP as the dependent variable and other variables as independent variables without time lag and with 10, 20 and 30 year time lags. From the regression result, it is understood that among the explanatory variables, GIAGCA variable was predominant and significant in influencing rural poverty, which was expected in the study. The coefficient of irrigation, which was represented by GIAGCA, was negatively and significantly associated with PRP in determining rural poverty. This shows that rural poverty is being determined by irrigation development. In short, the regression results demonstrated that except the irrigation variable, no other poverty determinant variables showed expected and significant results for all the time points. More importantly, irrigation (GIAGCA) significantly influenced the rural poverty with greater time lag. In other words, when the irrigation increased, it exercised tremendous impact on PRP.

Apart from irrigation, ELE, ROAD, CI, and GCAPTRP also determined the rural poverty. This implied that along with the irrigation, the other poverty determinants variables were also important in reducing rural poverty, under both with and without time lag settings.

8.6. Micro-level Analysis

The results of descriptive analysis of villages revealed that there was close association between source-wise irrigation and rural poverty.

The average employment days of agricultural labourers was higher in Groundwater Irrigated Village (GIV), followed by Canal Irrigated Village (CIV), Tank Irrigated Village (TIV) and Rainfed Village (RFV). Equally, Monthly Per Capita Income (MPI) of GIV was higher, followed by CIV, TIV and RFV. The Monthly Per Capita Consumption Expenditure (MPCE) was also more in GVI, followed by CIV, TIV and RFV. These indicate that the living standard of people in GIV was better than the CIV, TIV and RFV. Again, the living standard of people from CIV was better than TIV followed by RFV.

The number and percentage of households as well as population below poverty line were found to be more in un-irrigated areas than in the irrigated areas. Correspondingly, the number and percentage of households as well as population below poverty line was high in TIV than CIV. Again, number and percentage of households as well as population below poverty line were found largely in CIV as compared to GIV. This indicates that the impact of groundwater irrigation on rural poverty was more pronounced than the canal irrigation and tank irrigation. Likewise, canal irrigation was more pronounced in determining rural poverty than tank irrigation. In short, irrigation did influence poverty to a greater extent.

After acknowledging the impact of source-wise irrigation on rural poverty reduction from the descriptive analysis, different types of simple regressions were used to establish the independent relationship between source-wise irrigation and rural poverty (PPBPL) without considering any other poverty determinant variable. Simple regressions were computed by considering PPBPL (Percentage of Population Below Poverty Line) as the dependent variable and irrigation variable as independent variables. In order to represent irrigation variable in the analysis, D (DUMMY) was included as the irrigation variable. Results of different types of simple regression showed that groundwater irrigation significantly determined rural poverty. Next to the groundwater irrigation, canal irrigation was remarkable in determining rural poverty. The impact of tank irrigation on rural poverty was also identified which was also better than rainfed areas. However, it is pointed that the poverty-level was high in rainfed area as compared to the irrigated areas. On the whole, regression results revealed that there was strong inverse and significant relationship between irrigation and rural poverty which were expected from this study.

After analysing independent relationships among source-wise

irrigations and rural poverty, different types of multiple regression analysis were also performed because it is a known fact that rural poverty is determined by several factors. Multiple regressions analysis was carried out to identify which one of the irrigation source was more pronounced in determining rural poverty and also to study which of the selected poverty determinant variables played a major role in influencing rural poverty. Therefore, different types of multiple regressions were employed by considering PPBPL as the dependent variable and other poverty determinant variables as independent variables. The results of the different types of regressions showed that among the variables included for the analysis, groundwater irrigation was significant in determining the rural poverty. It was also found that among the irrigation sources, groundwater irrigation was the dominant factor in influencing rural poverty reduction. Further, next to the groundwater irrigation, the impact of canal irrigation was remarkable followed by tank irrigation, which was expected from this study.

Finally, the regression results, which was computed by treating PPBPL as the dependent variable and other poverty determinant variables as independent variables and treating irrigation as the DUMMY (D) variable (GIV=3, CIV=2, TIV=1 and RFV=0) revealed that among the poverty determinant factors, irrigation determined predominantly and significantly the rural poverty. Furthermore, there is a strong and significantly inverse relationship between irrigation and rural poverty in comparison to un-irrigated area. On the whole, the regression analysis suggested that irrigation variable appears to be the dominant factor in influencing the rural poverty.

In sum, State, district and micro-level analysis indicated that irrigation was the major factor in the reduction of rural poverty. The association of irrigation and poverty was strong, inverse and significant. The impact of base-level irrigation on rural poverty was also found to be remarkable across the State and districts.

8.7. Recommendations

Irrigation development appears to be the most important factor in determining the rural poverty, which was clearly demonstrated through this study. Keeping irrigation development as key for the poverty reduction, the study has made the following policy recommendations:

1. In most States where the incidence of poverty is high and the coverage of irrigation is low, there is a significant potentiality for its extension. Therefore, judicious policies should be formulated to utilise the untapped irrigation potential, wherever possible, on a priority basis. This is because the development of irrigation not only increases the production and productivity of agricultural commodities, but also helps to reduce the level of poverty through the percolation effect.
2. Improving water security should be the prime motto of the policymakers in order to have sustained reduction in rural poverty.
3. Due to high cost, small and marginal farmers are not able to install bore-wells, which affect their productivity and sustainability. Therefore, the Government must take steps to install public bore-wells to support the poor and resource less farmers. This will increase the standard of living of small and marginal farmers and reduce the number of poor.
4. To increase the benefits of irrigated agriculture to the poor, it is needed to understand the real social and economic benefits of irrigation development and the water environment where poor people live.
5. It was found that the incidence, depth, and severity of rural poverty were substantially lower in the irrigated ecosystem than in the rainfed ecosystem. Also that the income from all economic activities is much higher in irrigated ecosystem than in the rainfed. This is because irrigation technology contributed to higher income. Therefore, the adoption of modern irrigation technology and the expansion of reliable irrigation need to be developed on a war footing.
6. In order to enhance agricultural productivity and to accelerate the agricultural and rural economic growth, increased public investments in land and water resources development and management should be promoted.
7. The improved access to irrigation infrastructure has increased crop yield, agricultural production and farm income and in turn, reduces inequality and rural poverty within a region. Therefore, quality irrigation infrastructure is to be established. Further, extending access to irrigation to a large number of farmers and investing in human capital development are

crucial to increasing agricultural productivity and reducing poverty in India.

8. Water insecurity, erratic rainfall and low income from crop cultivation seem to be driving out the farmers and agriculture labourers from the agriculture sector. Therefore, it is necessary to increase the extent of irrigation coverage which is proved to reduce rural poverty, thereby preventing the farmers and agriculture labourers from abandoning their farm lands.
9. Agricultural extension and on-farm water management practices need to be promoted on a large scale in order to achieve increased and optimum crop production which could reduce rural poverty.
10. Minor irrigation (surface) sources, such as tanks, are very important for the resource-poor rural people in protecting their livelihood opportunities in many parts of India, particularly in Southern India. But, unfortunately, the area under tank irrigation, which is the most user friendly and cheapest source of irrigation, has been declining consistently since the introduction of new agricultural technology. Therefore, efforts are needed to repair, restore and renovate the small water bodies which besides being less capital-intensive are also the highly stable and reliable source of irrigation to the millions of small and marginal farmers.
11. Development of groundwater irrigation not only increases production and productivity of agricultural commodities but also increases the income of the agricultural labourers by giving more employment opportunities and helps to reduce the incidence of poverty. However, the over-exploitation of groundwater that is taking place in semi-arid and arid regions in India, can hamper the rate of reduction in poverty in rural areas. Therefore, stringent and well-designed policies need to be formulated to control this without harming agricultural growth.
12. Micro-irrigation systems, such as drip and sprinkler, have proved to save water and electricity substantially besides increasing productivity tremendously in various crops. These methods need to be aggressively promoted in those areas where over-exploitation of groundwater is a threat so as to reduce rural poverty in a sustained manner.

13. Development of groundwater irrigation not only increases production and productivity of agricultural commodities, but also increases the income of the agricultural labourers by giving more employment opportunities and helps to reduce the incidence of poverty. Therefore, long term policy should be formulated to utilize the untapped irrigation potential of the States.

On the whole, the policy-makers should prioritise irrigation development not only to increase the agricultural growth, but also as a strategy to alleviate the rural poverty on a sustained basis in India.

Bibliography

Abdullah, K.B. (2006), "Use of Water and Land for Food Security and Environmental Sustainability", *Irrigation and Drainage,* Vol. 55, No. 2, pp. 219-222.

Acharya, S. (1989), "Agricultural Wages in India: A Disaggregated Analysis", *Indian Journal of Agricultural Economics*, Vol. 44, No. 2, April-June, pp. 121-139.

Agarwal, A.G.; Bose, M.L. and Janaiah, A. (2000), "Poverty and Income Distribution in Rainfed and Irrigated Ecosystems", *Economic and Political Weekly,* Vol. 35, No. 52, December, pp. 4664-4669.

Ahluwalia, M.S. (1978), "Rural Poverty and Agricultural Performance in India", *Journal of Development Studies,* Vol. 14, No. 2, April, pp. 298-323.

Ahmad, M.U.D.; Bastiaanssen, W.G.M. and Feddes, R.A. (2003), "Sustainable Use of Groundwater for Irrigation: A Numerical Analysis of the Subsoil Water Fluxes", *Irrigation and Drainage,* Vol. 51, No. 3, pp. 227-241.

Asian Development Bank (2002), *Poverty in Pakistan: Issues, Causes and Institutional Responses*, ADB, Pakistan Resident Mission, Islamabad, Pakistan.

Banerjee, A. (1993), "The Impact of New Economic Policy on Agricultural Labour", *Indian Journal of Agricultural Economics*, Vol. 48, No. 3, July-September, pp. 471-476.

Bardhan, P.K. (1973), "Factors Affecting Wage Rates for Agricultural Labour", *Economic and Political Weekly*, Vol. 8, No. 26, June, pp. A56-A64.

Bardhan, P.K. and Mookherjee, D. (2004), "Poverty Alleviation Efforts of Panchayats in West Bengal", *Economic and Political Weekly,* Vol. 39, No. 9, February, pp. 965-974.

Bhalla, G.S. and Singh, G. (2010), *Growth of Indian Agriculture, Final Report on Planning Commission Project*, Centre for Study of Regional Development, Jawaharlal Nehru University, New Delhi, (www.planningcommission.nic.in).

Bhalla, G.S. and Singh, G. (2012), *Economic Liberalization and Indian Agriculture: A District-level Study*, Sage Publications India Private Limited, New Delhi.

Bhalla, S. (1987), "Trends in Employment in Indian Agriculture, Land and Asset Distribution", *Indian Journal of Agricultural Economics*, Vol. 42, No. 4, October-December, pp. 537-559.

Bhalla, S. (1993), "The Dynamics of Wage Determination and Employment Generation in Indian Agriculture", *Indian Journal of Agricultural Economics*, Vol. 48, No. 3, July-September, pp. 448-470.

Bhalla, S. (1995), "Development, Poverty and Policy: the Haryana Experience", *Economic and Political Weekly*, Vol. 30, Nos. 41-42, October, 1995. pp. 2619-2634.

Bhattarai, M. and Narayanamoorthy, A. (2003), "Impact of Irrigation on Rural Poverty in India: An Aggregate Panel—Data Analysis", *Water Policy*, Vol. 5, Nos. 5-6, pp. 443-458.

Bhattarai, M.; Barker, R. and Narayanamoorthy, A. (2007), "Who Benefits from Irrigation Development in India? Implication of Irrigation Multipliers for Irrigation Financing", *Irrigation and Drainage*, Vol. 56. Nos. 2-3, pp. 207 225.

Bhattarai, M.; Sakthivadivel, R. and Hussain, I. (2002), *Irrigation Impacts on Income Inequality and Poverty Alleviation: Policy Issues and Options for Improved Management of Irrigation Systems*, Working Paper 39, International Water Management Institute (IWMI), Colombo, Sri Lanka.

Binswanger, H.P.M. (2013), "The Stunted Structural Transformation of the Indian Economy: Agriculture, Manufacturing and the Rural Non-Farm Sector", *Economic and Political Weekly*, Vol. 58, Nos. 26-27, pp. 5-13.

Bohne, A.; Berlin, U. and Oktober (2008), *Agriculture, Agricultural Income and Rural Poverty in Malawi-Spatial Analysis of Determinants and Differences*, Beitrage zur Kölner Afrikawissenschaftlichen Nachwuchstagung (KANT II).

Bravo and Ureta, E.B. (2002), "Research Extension and Information: Key Inputs in Agricultural Productivity Growth", The *Pakistan Development Review*, Vol. 41, No. 4, pp. 48-52.

Census of India, (various years), *Office of the Registrar General and Census Commission*, Ministry of Home Affairs, Government of India, New Delhi.

Chadha, G.K. (2001), "Impact of Economic Reforms on Rural Employment: No Smooth Sailing Anticipated", *Indian Journal of Agricultural Economics*, Vol. 56, No. 3, July-September, pp. 491-525.

Chaudhuri, S. and Gupta, N. (2009), "Levels of Living and Poverty Patterns: A District-wise Analysis for India", *Economic and Political Weekly*, Vol. 44, No. 9, February, pp. 94-110.

Cook, S.E.; Fisher, M.J.; Harrington, L.W.; Lee, A.H. and Vidal, A. (2009), "Agricultural Water Productivity and Poverty: A Conceptual Pathway to Link Global, Basin and Local Understanding", *Irrigation and Drainage*, Vol. 58, No. 1, pp. S60-S72,

Coxhead, I. and Warr, P.G. (1995), "Does Technical Progress in Agriculture Alleviate Poverty? A Philippine Case Study", *Australian Journal of Agricultural Economics*, Vol. 39, No. 1, April, pp. 25-54.

Dandekar, V.M. and Rath, N. (1971), "Poverty in India—II Policies and Programmes", *Economic and Political Weekly*, Vol. 6, No. 2, January, pp. 106-145.

Datt, G. and Ravallion, M. (1996), *Why have some Indians States Done Better than Others at Reducing Rural Poverty?*, Policy Research Working Paper No. 1594, Policy Research Department, Poverty and Human Resources Division, the World Bank, Washington, D.C., U.S.A.

Datt, G. and Ravallion, M. (1998), "Farm Productivity and Rural Poverty in India", *The Journal of Development Studies*, Vol. 34, No. 4, pp. 62-85.

Desai, B.M. and Namboodiri, N.V. (1998), "Policy Strategy and Instruments for Alleviating Rural Poverty", *Economic and Political Weekly*, Vol. 33, No. 41, October, pp. 2669-2674.

Dethier, J.J. and Effenberger, A. (2011), *Agriculture and Development A Brief Review of the Literature*, Policy Research Working Paper 5553, Development Economics, World Bank.

Dev, S.M. (1988), "Poverty of Agricultural Labour Households in India: A State Level Analysis", *Indian Journal of Agricultural Economics*, Vol. 43, No. 1, January-March, pp. 14-25.

Dev, S.M. (1995), "Alleviating Poverty Maharashtra Employment Guarantee Scheme", *Economic and Political Weekly*, Vol. 30, Nos. 41-42, October, pp. 2663-2676.

Dhawan, B.D. (1988), *Irrigation in India's Agricultural Development: Productivity, Stability, Equity*, Sage Publications, New Delhi.

Dhawan, B.D. (1991), "Role of Irrigation in Raising Intensity of Cropping", *Journal of Indian School of Political Economy*, Vol. 3, No. 4, pp. 632-671.

Dollar, D. and Kraay, A. (2000), *Growth is Good for the Poor*, World Bank, Washington.

Dutta, P.; Murgai, R.; Ravallion, M.; and Walle, D. (2012), "Does India's Employment Guarantee Scheme Guarantee Employment?", *Economic and Political Weekly*, April, Vol. 47, No. 16, pp. 55-64.

Fan, S.; Hazaell, P.; and Thorat, S. (1999), *Linkages between Government Spending, Growth and Poverty in Rural India*, IFPRI Research Report No. 11, International Food Policy Research Institute, EPTD. Washington D.C.

Gandhi, V.P. and Namboodiri, N.V. (2009), *Groundwater Irrigation in India: Gains, Costs and Risks*, Working Paper No. 2009-03-08, Indian Institute of Management, Ahmedabad, India.

Gebrehaweria, G.; Regassa, N.E. and Stein, H. (2009), "Poverty Reduction with Irrigation Investment: An Empirical Case Study from Tigray, Ethiopia", *Agricultural Water Management*, Vol. 96, No. 12, pp. 1837-1843.

Ghosh, M. (1993), "Test of Trickle-Down Hypothesis in Rural West Bengal", *Indian Journal of Agricultural Economics*, Vol. 48, No. 2, April-June, pp. 215-225.

Ghosh, M. (1996), "Agricultural Development and Rural Poverty in India", *Indian Journal of Agricultural Economics*, Vol. 51, No. 3, July-September, pp. 374-380.

Ghosh, M. (1998), "Agricultural Development, Agrarian Structure and Rural Poverty in West Bengal", *Economic and Political Weekly*, Vol. 33, Nos. 47-48, November- December, pp. 2987-2995.

Ghosh, S. and Kumar, A. (2010), "Performance of Irrigation and Agricultural Sector in Odisha: An Analysis of Missing Links", *Indian Research Journal of Extension Education*, Vol. 10, No. 2, May, pp. 48-54.

Ghosh, S.; Panda, D.K.; Nanda, P. and Kumar, A. (2011), "Links between Irrigation, Agriculture and Level of Living", *Indian Research Journal of Extension Education*, Vol. 11, No. 3, September, pp. 32-36.

Ghosh, S.; Verma, H.C.; Panda, D.K.; Nanda, P. and Kumar, A. (2012), "Irrigation, Agriculture, Livelihood and Poverty Linkages in Odisha", *Agricultural Economics Research Review,* Vol. 25, No. 1, January-June, pp. 99-105.

Gill, Z.A. and Mustafa, M. (1997), "Farm-Area, Cultivated Area, and Irrigated Area Distribution in Pakistan, 1972-90", *Pakistan Journal of Agricultural Science*, Vol. 34, Nos. 1-4, pp. 98-101.

Government of India, (various years), *Agricultural Statistics at a Glance*, Director of Economics and Statistics, Department of Agricultural and Cooperation, Ministry of Agriculture, New Delhi.

Government of India, (various years), *Agricultural Wages in India*, Director of Economics and Statistics, Department of Agricultural and Cooperation, Ministry of Agriculture, New Delhi.

Government of Tamil Nadu (2013), *Department of Agriculture*, Aranthangi Taluk and Village Administrative Officers' Records (various village).

Hasnip, N.; Vincent, L. and Hussein, K. (1999), "Poverty Reduction and Irrigated Agriculture", IPTRID Issues Paper No. 1, Department for International Development, UK.

Hossain, M. and Sen, B. (1992), "Rural Poverty in Bangladesh: Trends and Determinants", *Asian Development Review*, Vol. 10, No. 1, pp. 85-91.

Hussain, I. (2004), *Assessing Impacts of Irrigation on Poverty: Approaches, Methods, Case Studies and Lessons*, Paper Presented at the Workshop, International Water Management Institute (IWMI), Colombo, Sri Lanka.

Hussain, I. (2007), "Direct and Indirect Benefits and Potential Disbenefits of Irrigation: Evidence and Lessons", *Irrigation and Drainage*, Vol. 56, Nos. 2-3, pp. 179-194.

Hussain, I. (2007b), "Pro-Poor Intervention Strategies in Irrigated Agriculture in Asia: Issues, Lessons, Options and Guidelines", *Irrigation and Drainage,* Vol. 56, Nos. 2-3, pp. 119-126.

Hussain, I. (2007c), "Poverty-Reducing Impacts of Irrigation: Evidence and Lessons", *Irrigation and Drainage,* Vol. 56, Nos. 2-3, pp. 147-164.

Hussain, I. and Biltonen, E. (2001), *Irrigation Against Rural Poverty: An Overview of Issues and Pro-Poor Intervention Strategies in Irrigated Agriculture in Asia*, ISBN 92-9090-450-X, International Water Management Institute, Colombo, Sri Lanka.

Hussain, I. and Hanjra, M.A. (2003), "Does Irrigation Water Matter for Rural Poverty Alleviation? Evidence from South and South-East Asia", *Water Policy*, Vol. 5, No. 5, pp. 429-442.

Hussain, I. and Hanjra, M.A. (2004), "Irrigation and Poverty Alleviation: Review of the Empirical Evidence", *Irrigation and Drainage*, Vol. 53, No. 2, pp. 1-15.

Hussain, I. and Wijerathna, D. (2004), *Irrigation and Income—Poverty Alleviation: A Comparative Analysis of Irrigation Systems in Developing Asia*, Research report 62, International Water Management Institute (IWMI), Colombo, Sri Lanka.

Hussain, I.; Fuard, M. and Sunil, T. (2002), *Assessment of Impact of Irrigation Infrastructure Development on Poverty Alleviation*, Sri Lanka Component, Colombo, IWMI.

Hussain, I.; Gichuki, F.; Louw, M.A.; Andah, W. and Moustafa, M. (2007), "Agricultural Water Management Pathways to Breaking the Poverty Trap: Case Studies of the Limpopo, Nile and Volta River Basins", *Irrigation and Drainage*, Vol. 56, Nos. 2-3, pp. 277-288.

Hussain, I.; Giordano, M. and Hanjra, M.A. (2003), "Agricultural Water and Poverty Linkages: Case Studies on Large and Small Systems", *Water and Poverty*, Vol. 5, No. 1, pp. 52-73.

Hussain, M.; Hussain, Z. and Ashfaq, M. (2006), "Impact of Small Scale Irrigation Schemes on Poverty Alleviation, in Marginal Areas of Punjab, Pakistan", *International Research Journal of Finance and Economics*, Vol. 6, No. 6, pp. 1-15.

Janvry, A.D. and Sadoulet, E. (2001), "World Poverty and the Role of Agricultural Technology: Direct and Indirect Effects", *Journal of Development Studies*, Vol. 38, No. 4, pp. 1-26.

Janvry, A.D. and Sadoulet, E. (2010), "Agricultural Growth and Poverty Reduction: Additional Evidence", *The World Bank Research Observer*, Vol. 25, No. 1, February, pp. 2-20.

Janvry, A.D.; Sadoulet, E. and Zhu, N. (2005), the *Role of Non-farm Incomes in Reducing Rural Poverty and inequality in China*, CUDARE working paper series 100, Department of Agricultural and Resource Economics and Policy University of California, Berkeley.

Jatav, M. and Sen, S. (2013), "Drivers of Non-Farm Employment in Rural India: Evidence from the 2011-12 NSSO Round", *Economic and Political Weekly*, Vol. 58, Nos. 26-27, pp. 14-21.

Jonna, P.E. and Keijiro, O. (2010), *Rural Poverty and Income Dynamics in Southeast Asia*, Handbook of Agricultural Economics, Elsevier, Vol. 4, No. 1, pp. 6-67.

Jose, A.V. (1973), "Wage Rates of Agricultural Labourers in Kerala", *Economic and Political Weekly*, Vol. 8, Nos. 4-5-6, February, pp. 281-288.

Jose, A.V. (1988), "Agricultural Wages in India", *Economic and Political Weekly*, Vol. 23, No. 26, June 25, pp. A46-A58.

Kalman, K.P. (1995), "Declining Incidence of Rural Poverty in Kerala", *Economic and Political Weekly*, Vol. 30, Nos. 41-42, October, pp. 2651-2662.

Kalpana, (1973), "Factors Affecting Wage Rates for Agricultural Labour", *Economic and Political Weekly,* Vol. 8, No. 26, June 30, pp. A57-A64.

Kerr, J.M. (1996), *Sustainable Development of Rainfed Agriculture in India,* EPTD Discussion Paper No. 20, International Food Policy Research Institute, Washington, U.S.A.

Khan, A.R. (2007), *Growth, Employment and Poverty: An Analysis of the Vital Nexus based on some Recent UNDP and ILO/SIDA Studies,* DESA Working Paper No. 49, ST/ESA/2007/DWP/49.

Khan, M.H., (1997), "Economic Performance, Structural Reforms and Government Budgets in Pakistan", *Canadian Journal of Development Studies,* Vol. 18, No. 2, pp. 87-95.

Kumar, T.K. (1993), "Measures of Poverty Suited to Design and Evaluate Poverty Alleviation Programme", *Economic and Political Weekly,* Vol. 28, No. 52, December, pp. 2893-2895.

Lal, D. (1976), "Agricultural Growth, Real Wages and the Rural Poor in India", *Economic and Political Weekly,* Vol. 11, No. 26, June, pp. A47-A61.

Laurence E.D. Smith (2004), "Assessment of the Contribution of Irrigation to Poverty Reduction and Sustainable Livelihoods", *International Journal of Water Resources Development,* Vol. 20, No. 2, June, pp. 243-257.

Lipton, M. (1977), *Why Poor People Stay Poor: Urban Bias in World Development,* Temple Smith, London.

Lipton, M. (2007), "Farm Water and Rural Poverty Reduction in Developing Asia", *Irrigation and Drainage,* Vol. 56, pp. 127-146.

Lipton, M.; Litchfield, J. and Faures, J.M. (2002), "The Effects of Irrigation on Poverty: A Framework for Analysis", *Water Policy,* Vol. 5, No. 5, pp. 413-427.

Luc, C.; Lionel, D. and Jesper, K. (2006), *The Role of Agriculture in Poverty Reduction an Empirical Perspective,* Policy Research Working Paper 4013, World Bank.

Magistro, J.; Roberts, M.; Haggblade, S.; Kramer, F.; Polak, P.; Weight, E. and Yoder, R. (2007), "A Model for Pro-poor Wealth Creation through Small-Plot Irrigation and Market Linkages", *Irrigation and Drainage,* Vol. 56, Nos. 2-3, pp. 321-334.

Mellor, J.W. (1985), *Determinants of Rural Poverty: The Dynamics of Production, Technology, and Price,* Agricultural Change and Rural Poverty: Variation on a Theme by Dharm Narain, In: Mellor, J.W. and Desai, G.M. (eds.), The Johns Hopkins University Press, Baltimore, MD. pp. 21-40.

Mellor, J.W. (1996), "Accelerating Agricultural Growth—Is Irrigation Institutional Reforms Necessary", *The Pakistan Development Review,* Vol. 35: No. 4, pp. 399-417.

Mellor, J.W. (2001), "Irrigation Agriculture and Poverty Reduction: General Relationships and Specific Needs," Managing Water for Poor: Workshop Proceedings, 9-10 August, 2001, In: Hussain, I. and Biltonen, E. (eds.), *International Water Management Institute (IWMI),* Colombo, Sri Lanka. pp. 53-69.

Molden, D.; Burton, M. and Bos, M.G. (2007), "Performance Assessment, Irrigation Service Delivery and Poverty Reduction: Benefits of Improved

System Management", *Irrigation and Drainage,* Vol. 56, Nos. 2-3, pp. 307-320.

Nadkarni, M.V. (1984), "Irrigation and Rural Development", *Economic and Political Weekly,* Vol. 19, No. 26, June, pp. A67-A73.

Narayanamoorthy, A. (1994), "Who Sells More and Who Sells Less in Deep Bore-Well Water Business in Pudukkottai District, Tamil Nadu: Some Empirical Analysis", *Journal of Indian Water Resources Society*, Vol. 14, Nos. 1-4, January-October, pp. 51-56.

Narayanamoorthy, A. (1996), "Electric Pumpset and Groundwater Management: Macro and Micro-Evidence of India", *Water Resources Journal*, No. 189, June, pp. 24-33.

Narayanamoorthy, A. (2001), "Irrigation and Rural Poverty Nexus: A State-wise Analysis", *Indian Journal of Agricultural Economics*, Vol. 56, No. 1, pp. 40-56.

Narayanamoorthy, A. (2007), "Does Groundwater Irrigation Reduce Rural Poverty? Evidence from Indian States", *Irrigation and Drainage*, Vol. 56, No. 2-3, pp. 349-362.

Narayanamoorthy, A. (2007), "Tank Irrigation in India: A Time Series Analysis", *Water Policy,* Vol. 9, No. 2, pp. 193-216.

Narayanamoorthy, A. (2010), "India's Groundwater Irrigation Boom: Can it be Sustained?", *Water Policy*, Vol. 12, No. 4, pp. 543-563.

Narayanamoorthy, A. and Deshpande, R.S. (2003), "Irrigation Development and Agricultural Wages: An Analysis across States", *Economic and Political Weekly,* Vol. 38, No. 35, pp. 3716-3722.

Narayanamoorthy, A. and Hanjra, M.A. (2006), "Rural Infrastructure and Agriculture Output Linkages: A Study of256 Indian Districts", *Indian Journal of Agricultural Economics*, Vol. 61, No. 3, pp. 444-459.

Narayanamoorthy, A. and Hanjra, M.A. (2010), "What Contributes to Disparity in Rural-Urban Poverty in Tamil Nadu?: A District Level Analysis", *Indian Journal of Agricultural Economics*, Vol. 65, No. 2, pp. 228-244.

Nayak, S. (2009), "Distributional Inequality and Groundwater Depletion: An Analysis across Major States in India", *Indian Journal of Agricultural Economics*, Vol. 64, No. 1, January-March, pp. 89-107.

Nayyar, R. (1996), "New Initiatives for Poverty Alleviations in Rural India", In: *Economic Reforms and Poverty Alleviation in India*, C.H.H. Rao and H. Linnemann (Eds.), Sage Publications, New Delhi, pp. 171-198.

Palmer, R.W. Jones (1992), "Groundwater Irrigation, Growth of Agricultural Production and Poverty in Bangladesh", *Economic and Political Weekly*, Vol. 27, No. 39, September, pp. A128-A140.

Palmer, R.W. and Sen, K. (2003), "What has Luck Got to do with it? A Regional Analysis of Poverty and Agricultural Growth in Rural India", *The Journal of Development Studies*, Vol. 40, No. 1, pp. 31-37.

Pandey, P. and Reddy, A.A. (2012), "Farm Productivity and Rural Poverty in Uttar Pradesh: A Regional Perspective", *Agricultural Economics Research Review,* Vol. 25, No. 1, January-June, pp. 25-35.

Pandey, R.K. and Kumar, A. (1993), "Economic Study of Agricultural Wages, Output and Productivity in Odisha", *Indian Journal of Agricultural Economics*, Vol. 48, No. 3, July-September, pp. 477-487.

Pant, N. (1998), "Indigenous Irrigation in South Bihar: A Case of Congruence of Boundaries", *Economic and Political Weekly*, Vol. 33, No. 49, December, pp. 3132-3138.

Parthasarathy, G. (1995), "Public Intervention and Rural Poverty", *Economic and Political Weekly*, Vol. 30, Nos. 41-42, October, pp. 2573-2586.

Parthasarathy, G. (1996), "Recent Trends in Wages and Employment of Agricultural Labour", *Indian Journal of Agricultural Economics*, Vol. 51, Nos. 1-2, pp. 145-167.

Patnaik, U. (2007), "Neoliberalism and Rural Poverty in India", *Economic and Political Weekly*, Vol. 42, No. 30, July, pp. 3132-3150.

Paul, S. (1990), "Green Revolution and Poverty among Farm Families in Haryana, 1969/70-1982", *Economic and Political Weekly*, Vol. 25, No. 39, September, pp. A105-A110.

Planning Commission, (2013), *Report of the Expert Group to Review the Methodology for Estimation of Poverty*, Government of India, New Delhi, (www.planningcommission.nic.in).

Planning Commission, (2014), *Report of the Expert Group to Review the Methodology for Estimation of Poverty*, Government of India, New Delhi, (www.planningcommission.nic.in).

Rao, C.H.H. (1972), "Agricultural Growth and Rural Poverty—Some Lessons from Past Experience", *Economic and Political Weekly*, Vol. 12, No. 33, November, pp. 162-173.

Rao, C.H.H. (1973), "Strategy for Removal of Poverty—Lopsidedness of Fifth Plan Approach", *Economic and Political Weekly*, Vol. 8, No. 31, December, pp. 1465-1466.

Rao, C.H.H. (1987), "Poverty Alleviation Programmes and the Poor", *Economic and Political Weekly*, Vol. 22, No. 35, August, p. 1491.

Rao, C.H.H. (1992), "Integrating Poverty Alleviation Programmes with Development Strategies", *Economic and Political Weekly*, Vol. 27, No. 48, November, pp. 2603-2607.

Rao, V.M. (1978), "Linking Irrigation with Development", *Economic and Political Weekly*, Vol. 13, No. 24, June, pp. 993-997.

Rath, N. (1985), "Garibi Hatao: Can IRDP Do It?", *Economic and Political Weekly*, Vol. 20, No. 6, February, pp. 238-246.

Rath, N. (1996), "Poverty in India Revisited", *Indian Journal of Agricultural Economics*, Vol. 51, Nos. 1 and 2, January-June, pp. 76-108.

Rath, N. and Mitra, A.K. (1989), "Economics of Irrigation in Water Scare Region: A Study of Maharashtra", *Artha Vijnana*, Vol. 31, No. 1, March, pp. 1-129.

Rath, S. (2007), "Employment, Income and Food Intake of Poor", *Journal of Indian School of Political Economy*, Vol. 9, No. 4, October-December, pp. 597-647.

Ravallion, M. and Datt, G. (1996), "India's Checkered History in Fight Against Poverty are There Lessons for the Future?", *Economic and Political Weekly*, Vol. 31, Nos. 35-37, September, pp. 176-178.

Ray, S.K. (1992), "Development of Irrigation and Its Impact of Pattern of Land Use, Output Growth and Employment Generation", *Journal of Indian School of Political Economy*, Vol. 4, No. 4, pp. 677-700.

Reddy, M.V. (1995), "Sociology of Major Irrigation in India–Some Dimensions", *Man and Development*, Vol. 17, No. 4, December, pp. 57-74.

Reddy, T.P. (2004), "Falling into Poverty in AP", *Economic and Political Weekly*, Vol. 39, No. 41, October, pp. 4482.

Rijsberman, F. (2003), "Can Development of Water Resources Reduce Poverty?" *Water Policy*, Vol. 5. No. 5, pp. 399-412.

Sagar, V. (1995), "Public Intervention for Poverty Alleviation in Harsh Agro-Climatic Environment", *Economic and Political Weekly*, Vol. 30, No. 41, October, pp. 2677-2690.

Sah, D.C. (2007), "Chronic Poverty in Tribal Areas: Evidence from Southwestern Madhya Pradesh", *Indian Journal of Agricultural Economics*, Vol. 62, No. 2, April-June, pp. 193-215.

Saleth, R.M.; Namara, R.E. and Samad, M. (2003), "Dynamics of Irrigation—Poverty Linkages in Rural India: Analytical Framework and Empirical Analysis", *Water Policy*, Vol. 5, No. 5, pp. 459-473.

Samal, K.C. (1998), "Poverty Alleviation after Post-Liberalization: Study of a Tribal Block in Odisha", *Economic and Political Weekly*, Vol. 33, No. 28, July, pp. 1846-1857.

Schultz, B.; Tardieu, H. and Vida, A. (2009), "Role of Water Management for Global Food Production and Poverty Alleviation", *Irrigation and Drainage*, Vol. 58, No. 1, pp. S3-S21.

Schultz, B.; Thatte, C.D. and Labhsetwar, V.K. (2005), "Irrigation and Drainage: Main Contributors to Global Food Production", *Irrigation and Drainage*, Vol. 54, No. 3, pp. 263-278.

Shah, T. (1993), "Ground Water Markets and Irrigation Development", *Political Economy and Practical Policy*, Oxford University Press.

Shah, T. and Raju, K.V. (1988), "Groundwater Markets and Small Farmer Development", *Economic and Political Weekly*, Vol. 23, No. 13, pp. A23-A28.

Shah, T. and Singh, O.P. (2004), "Irrigation Development and Rural Poverty in Gujarat, India: A Disaggregated Analysis", *Water International*, Vol. 29, No. 2, pp. 167-177.

Sharma, A.N. (1995), "Political Economy of Poverty in India", *Economic and Political Weekly*, Vol. 30, Nos. 41-42, October, pp. 2587-2602.

Sharma, S.R. (2002), "Irrigation", *Economic History of India*: 1857-1956, V.B. Singh, (Ed.), Allied Publishers Private Limited, New Delhi, pp. 162-180.

Shergill, H.S. and Singh, G. (1995), "Poverty in Rural Punjab: Trend over Green Revolution Decades", *Economic and Political Weekly*, Vol. 30, No, 25, June, pp. A80-A83.

Simon, E.C.; Myles, J.F.; Meike, S.A.; Jorge, R. and Mark, G. (2009), "Water, Food and Livelihoods in River Basins", *Water International*, Vol. 34, No. 1, March, pp. 13-29.

Skaggs, R.K. and Samani, Z. (2005), "Farm Size, Irrigation Practices, and On-farm Irrigation Efficiency, *Irrigation and Drainage*, Vol. 54, No. 1, pp. 43-57.

Smith, L.E.D. (2004), "Assessment of the Contribution of Irrigation to Poverty Reduction and Sustainable Livelihoods", *Water Resources Development*, Vol. 20, No. 2, June, pp. 243-257.

Subramanian, S.R. (1993), "Reporter's Report on Agricultural Wages and Employment", *Indian Journal of Agricultural Economics*, Vol. 48, No. 3, July-September, pp. 599-604.

Sundaram, K. and Tendulkar, S.D. (1983), "Poverty in the Mid", *Economic and Political Weekly*, Vol. 18, No. 45, November, pp. 1982-1934.

Sundaram, K. and Tendulkar, S.D. (1988), "Towards an Explanation of Interregional Variation in Poverty and Unemployment in Rural India", In: *Rural Poverty in South Asia*, T.N. Srinivasan and Pranab K. Bardhan, (Eds.), Oxford University Press, Delhi, pp. 316-362.

Tendulkar, S.D. and Jain, L.R. (1995), "Economic Reforms and Poverty", *Economic and Political Weekly*, Vol. 30, No. 23, June, pp. 1373-1383.

Tendulkar, S.D. and Jain, L.R. (1996), "Growth, Distributional Change and Reduction in Rural Poverty between 1983 and 1987-88: A Decomposition Exercise for Seventeen States in India", *Indian Journal of Agricultural Economics*, Vol. 51, Nos. 1 and 2, January-June, pp. 108-133.

Thirtle, C. and Piesse, J. (2007), "Governance, Agricultural Productivity and Poverty Reduction in Africa, Asia and Latin America", *Irrigation and Drainage*, Vol. 56, Nos. 2-3, pp. 165-177.

Thirtle, C.; Xavier, I.; Lin, L.; McKenzie-Hill, C. and Wiggins, S. (2001), *Relationship between Changes in Agricultural Productivity and the Incidence of Poverty in Developing Countries,* DFID, London.

Thorat, S. and Fan, S. (2007), "Public Investment and Poverty Reduction: Lessons from China and India", *Economic and Political Weekly,* Vol. 42. No. 8, February, pp. 704-710.

Timmer, C.P. (1997), *How Well Do the Poor Connect to the Growth Process*, CAER II Discussion Paper No. 17, Harward Institute of International Development, Cambridge, USA.

United Nations Development Programme, (1990), *Human Development Report*, New York.

Vaidyanathan, A. (1994), "Employment Situation: Some Emerging Perspectives", *Economic and Political Weekly*, Vol. 29, No. 50, December, pp. 3147-3156.

Vaidyanathan, A. (1996), "Depletion of Groundwater: Some Issues", *Indian Journal of Agricultural Economics,* Vol. 51, Nos. 1-2, pp. 184-192.

Vaidyanathan, A. (1995), "Making Poverty Research More Relevant", *Economic and Political Weekly,* Vol. 30, No. 46, November, pp. 2929-2931.

Vaidyanathan, A., Kumar, A.K., Rajagopal, A. and Varatharajan, D. (1994), "Impact of Irrigation on Productivity of Land", *Journal of Indian School of Political Economy,* Vol. 6, No. 4, pp. 601–645.

Visaria, P. and Basant, R. (1994), *Non-Agricultural Employment in India: Trends and Prospects,* Sage Publications, New Delhi.

Vyas, V.S. and Bhargava, P. (1995), "Public Intervention for Poverty Alleviation: An Overview", *Economic and Political Weekly,* Vol. 30, No. 41, October, pp. 2559-2572.

Wiggins, S. (2001), *Spatial Dimensions of Rural Development*, Department of Agricultural and Food Economics, University of Reading.

Index